PRAISE FOR DREAMS
NO. 1 NEW YORK TIMES

"YOU'RE GUARANTEED TO WALK AWAY INSPIRED."
Marcus Rashford

"An American classic, written with grace and precision."
OBSERVER

"EXTRAORDINARY... It's unique. It's his. There are no other ones like that."
Toni Morrison

"Provocative... Persuasively describes the phenomenon of belonging to two different worlds, and thus belonging to neither."
NEW YORK TIMES BOOK REVIEW

OFFALY LIBRARIES

"THOUGHTFUL, MOVING and BRILLIANTLY WRITTEN."
The Times

"Obama is a BORN NARRATOR."
Sunday Times

"A well-written account of Obama's struggle to establish his own views on identity and race, and all the more entertaining for its honesty."
FINANCIAL TIMES

"Fluidly, calmly, insightfully, Obama guides us straight to the intersection of the most serious questions of identity, class, and race."
WASHINGTON POST BOOK WORLD

"You will not fail to be moved by OBAMA'S WARMTH AND HUMILITY."
Good Book Guide

ALSO BY BARACK OBAMA

A Promised Land

The Audacity of Hope

Dreams from My Father (adult edition)

DREAMS
FROM MY
FATHER

A STORY OF RACE AND INHERITANCE

ADAPTED FOR YOUNG ADULTS

BARACK
OBAMA

**WALKER
BOOKS**

This edition published 2022 by Walker Books Ltd
87 Vauxhall Walk, London SE11 5HJ

Published by arrangement with Canongate Books Ltd, Edinburgh

First published in the United States by Delacorte Press,
an imprint of Random House Children's Books, a division
of Penguin Random House LLC, New York

2 4 6 8 10 9 7 5 3 1

Interior design by Stephanie Moss
Jacket design by Christopher Brand
Family tree designed by Barbara M. Bachman

Interior photograph credits appear on pages 343–4

This book has been typeset in Minion Pro

Printed and bound by CPI Group (UK) Ltd, Croydon CR0 4YY

British Library Cataloguing in Publication Data:
a catalogue record for this book is available from the British Library

ISBN 978-1-4063-3447-0

www.walker.co.uk

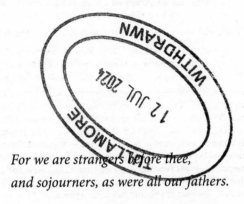

For we are strangers before thee,
and sojourners, as were all our fathers.

1 Chronicles 29:15

THE OBAMA FAMILY TREE

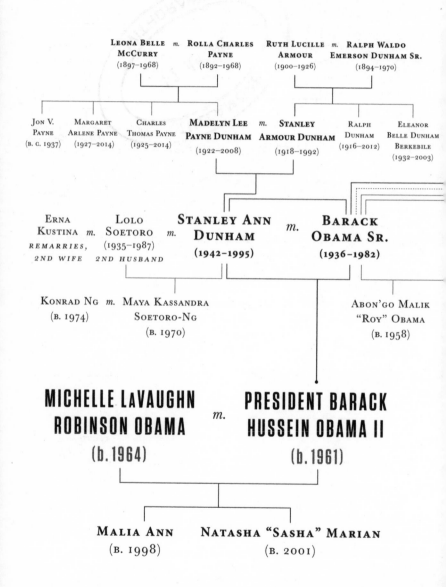

LEONA BELLE **m.** ROLLA CHARLES — RUTH LUCILLE **m.** RALPH WALDO
McCURRY — PAYNE — ARMOUR — EMERSON DUNHAM SR.
(1897–1968) — (1892–1968) — (1900–1926) — (1894–1970)

JON V. — MARGARET — CHARLES — **MADELYN LEE** **m.** **STANLEY** — RALPH — ELEANOR
PAYNE — ARLENE PAYNE — THOMAS PAYNE — **PAYNE DUNHAM** **ARMOUR DUNHAM** — DUNHAM — BELLE DUNHAM
(B. C. 1937) — (1927–2014) — (1925–2014) — **(1922–2008)** — **(1918–1992)** — (1916–2012) — BERKEBILE
(1932–2003)

ERNA — LOLO — **STANLEY ANN** **m.** **BARACK**
KUSTINA **m.** SOETORO **m.** **DUNHAM** — **OBAMA SR.**
REMARRIES, (1935–1987) — **(1942–1995)** — **(1936–1982)**
2ND WIFE *2ND HUSBAND*

KONRAD NG **m.** MAYA KASSANDRA — ABON'GO MALIK
(B. 1974) — SOETORO-NG — "ROY" OBAMA
(B. 1970) — (B. 1958)

MICHELLE LaVAUGHN ROBINSON OBAMA (b. 1964)
m.
PRESIDENT BARACK HUSSEIN OBAMA II (b. 1961)

MALIA ANN — NATASHA "SASHA" MARIAN
(B. 1998) — (B. 2001)

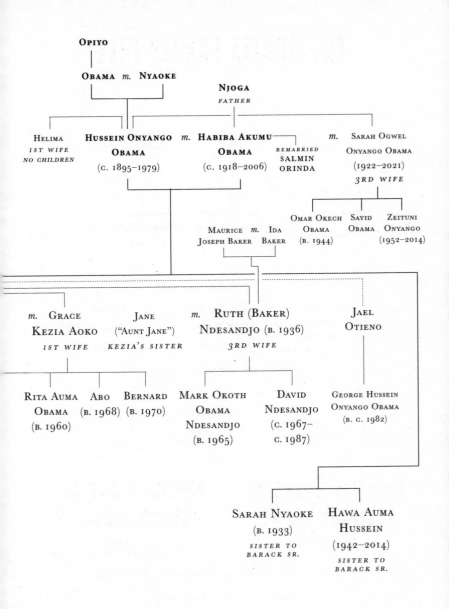

INTRODUCTION

was in my early thirties when I wrote *Dreams from My Father*. At the time, I was a few years out of law school. Michelle and I were newly married and just beginning to think about having kids. My mother was still alive. And I was not yet a politician.

I look back now and understand that I was at an important crossroads then, thinking hard about who I wanted to be in the world and what sort of contribution I could make. I was passionate about civil rights, curious about public service, full of loose ideas, and entirely uncertain about which path I should take. I had more questions than answers. Was it possible to create more trust between people and lessen our divides? How much did small steps toward progress matter—improving conditions at a school, say, or registering more people to vote—when our larger systems seemed so broken? Would I accomplish more by working inside existing institutions or outside of them?

Behind all of this floated something more personal, a deeper set of unresolved questions: Who am I? Where do I come from? How do I belong?

That's what compelled me to start writing this book.

I've always believed that the best way to meet the future involves making an earnest attempt at understanding the past. It's why I enjoy reading different accounts of history and why I value the insights of those who've been on this earth longer than I have. Some folks might see history as something we put behind us, a bunch of words and dates carved in stone, a set of dusty artifacts best stored in a vault. But for me, history is alive the same way an old-growth forest is alive, deep and rich, rooted and branching off in unexpected directions, full of shadows and light. What matters most is how we carry ourselves through that forest—the perspectives we bring, the assumptions we make, and our willingness to keep returning to it, to ask the harder questions about what's been ignored, whose voices have been erased.

These pages represent my early, earnest attempt to walk through my own past, to examine the strands of my heritage as I considered my future. In writing it, I was able to dwell inside the lives of my parents and grandparents, the landscapes, cultures, and histories they carried, the values and judgments that shaped them—and that in turn shaped me. What I learned through this process helped to ground me. It became the basis for how I moved forward, giving me the confidence to know I could be a good father to my children and the courage to know I was ready to step forward as a leader.

The act of writing is exactly that powerful. It's a chance to be inquisitive with yourself, to observe the world, confront your limits, walk in the shoes of others, and try on new ideas. Writing is difficult, but that's kind of the point. You might spend hours pushing yourself to remember what an old classroom smelled like, or the timbre of your father's voice, or the precise color of some shells you saw once on a beach. This work can anchor you, and fortify you, and surprise you. In finding the right words, in putting in that time, you may not always hit upon specific answers to life's big questions, but you will understand yourself better. That's how it works for me, anyway.

The young man you meet in these pages is flawed and full of yearning, asking questions of himself and the world around him, learning as he goes. I know now, of course, that this was just the beginning for him. If you're lucky, life provides you with a good long arc. I hope that my story will encourage you to think about telling your story, and to value the stories of others around you. The journey is always worth taking. Your answers will come.

Barack Obama
JUNE 2021

DREAMS

FROM MY

FATHER

PART ONE

ORIGINS

CHAPTER 1

barely knew my father. He left our home in Hawaii back in 1963, when I was only two. I didn't even know I was supposed to have a father who lived with his family. All I knew were the stories that my mother and grandparents told.

They had their favorites. I can still picture Gramps leaning back in his old stuffed chair, laughing about the time my father—whose name, like mine, was Barack Obama—almost threw a man off the Pali Lookout, a mountain cliff not far from our home in the city of Honolulu, because of a pipe.

"See, your mom and dad decided to drive this visiting friend around the island—and Barack was probably on the wrong side of the road the whole way—"

"Your father was a terrible driver," my mother said to me. "He'd end up on the left side, the way the British drive, and if you said something he'd just huff about silly American rules—"

"And they got out and stood at the railing of this cliff to admire the view. And your father, he was puffing away on this pipe that I'd given him for his birthday, pointing out all the sights with the stem like a sea captain—"

"He was really proud of this pipe," my mother interrupted again.

"Look, Ann, do you want to tell the story or are you going to let me finish?"

"Sorry, Dad. Go ahead."

"Anyway, the fella asked Barack if he could give the pipe a try. But as soon as he took his first puff, he started coughing up a fit. Coughed so hard that the pipe slipped out of his hand and dropped over the railing, a hundred feet down the face of the cliff. So your dad told him to climb over the railing and bring the pipe back."

Gramps was laughing so hard he had to pause. "The man took one look over the side and said he'd buy him a replacement. But Barack said it had been a gift and it couldn't be replaced. That's when your dad picked him clear off the ground and started dangling him over the railing!"

As he laughed, I imagined myself looking up at my father, dark against the brilliant sun, the man's arms flailing. It was like something out of the Bible—a terrifying yet impressive vision, like a king delivering justice.

I asked if he'd thrown the man off.

"No, he put him down," said Gramps. "After a time. Then your dad patted him on the back and suggested, calm as you please, that they all go have a beer. After that he acted like nothing had happened."

My mother said it wasn't that bad, that my father didn't hold the man very far out.

"You were pretty upset when you got home," Gramps told my mother. "But Barack just shook his head and started to laugh. He had this deep voice, see, and this British accent. He said, 'I only wanted to teach the chap a lesson about the proper care of other people's property!'"

My grandmother, Toot, came in from the kitchen and said it was a good thing my father had realized that his friend dropping the pipe had been an accident—or who knows what would have happened?

My mother rolled her eyes and said they were exaggerating. Yes, she said, my father could be domineering, but only because he was honest. "If he thought he was right, he never liked to compromise," she said.

She preferred another story Gramps told, about the time my father agreed to sing some African songs at an international music festival, not realizing it was a "big to-do." It turned out that the woman who performed just before him was a pro with a full band. "Anyone else would have backed out," said Gramps. "But not Barack. He got up and started singing in front of this big crowd—which is no easy feat, let me tell you—and he wasn't great, but he was so sure of himself that before you knew it he was getting as much applause as anybody."

"Now there's something you can learn from your dad," he would tell me. "*Confidence*. The secret to a man's success."

THAT'S HOW ALL the stories went—short, with some tidy moral. Then my family would pack them away like old photos and take them out again, months or years later. My mother kept a few actual photos of my father, too. But when she started dating Lolo, the man she'd eventually marry, she put them in a closet. Every once in a while I'd be rummaging around in search of Christmas ornaments or an old snorkel set, and I'd come across them. Sometimes my mother and I looked at them together. I'd stare at my father's likeness—the dark laughing face, the big forehead and thick glasses—and she'd say, "You have me to thank for your big eyebrows— your father has these little wispy ones. But your brains, your character, you got from him."

I would listen as she told me his story.

My father was an African, a Kenyan who'd grown up in a tribe called the Luos. He was born on the shores of Lake Victoria in a place called Alego. The village of Alego was poor, but his father—my other grandfather—was an elder of the Luo tribe and a powerful medicine man. My father grew up herding his father's goats and attending the local school, which had been set up by the British colonialists, who at that time ruled Kenya.

My grandfather believed that knowledge was the source

of power, so he was pleased that Barack showed great promise as a student and won a scholarship to study in the capitol, Nairobi. Then he was selected by Kenyan leaders and American sponsors to go to college in the United States. Kenya was about to become an independent country, and the new leaders sent their best students abroad to learn about economics and technology. They hoped these students would come back home and help make Africa more modern and successful.

In 1959, at the age of twenty-three, my father arrived at the University of Hawaii to study economics. He was the first African student there and he graduated in only three years, and at the top of his class. He helped organize the International Students Association and became its first president. Then, in a Russian language course, he met an awkward, shy American girl, only eighteen, and they fell in love. Her name was Stanley Ann Dunham, but everyone called her Ann. She was my mother.

Her parents were not sure about him at first. He was Black and she was white, and it was not common back then for people of different races to date. But he won them over with his charm and intelligence. The young couple married, and a short time later, I was born.

Then my father was awarded yet another scholarship, this time to get a Ph.D. at Harvard University, more than five thousand miles away in Cambridge, Massachusetts, but he had no money to take his new family with him. We stayed behind. After getting his degree, he returned to Africa—"to make his country a better place," my mother would say. But she insisted that the bond of love remained strong.

There were many parts to this story that I didn't understand. I didn't know where Alego was on a map or why the British were in charge in Kenya or what a Ph.D. was. My father's life seemed as mysterious as the stories in a book called *Origins* my mother once bought for me. It was a collection of tales from different religions and from all over the world—Christian, Jewish, ancient Greek, Indian—about the Earth's creation, and it led me to ask some difficult questions. Why did God let the snake make such trouble in the Garden of Eden? How did the tortoise from the Hindu stories support the weight of the world on its tiny back? Why didn't my father return?

I spent my boyhood living with my mother and grand-parents, Stanley and Madelyn Dunham, Gramps and Toot. Toot is short for Tutu, which means "grandmother" in Hawaiian. Toot decided on the day I was born that she was still too young to be called Granny.

I loved Hawaii. I breathed it all in: The sultry scented air. The shimmering blue Pacific. The moss-covered cliffs and the cool rush of Manoa Falls, with its ginger blossoms and high canopies filled with the sound of invisible birds. The North Shore's thunderous waves, so huge that when they broke it seemed I was watching the ocean in slow motion.

There was only one problem: my father was missing. And

nothing that my mother or grandparents told me could make me forget that fact. Their stories didn't tell me why he had left. And they couldn't describe what it might have been like had he stayed.

In photographs, I could see that my father looked nothing like the people around me—he was black as pitch, my mother white as milk. But it wasn't something we talked about, and it didn't really register in my mind.

In fact, I remember only one story about my father that had anything to do with race. After long hours of study, my father had joined my grandfather and several other friends at a local bar in the beachfront area of Waikiki. Everyone was in a festive mood, eating and drinking to the sounds of a Hawaiian slack-key guitar, when a white man abruptly announced to the bartender, loudly enough for everyone to hear, that he shouldn't have to drink good liquor "next to a nigger." The room fell quiet and people turned to my father, expecting a fight. Instead, my father stood up, walked over to the man, smiled, and proceeded to lecture him about the foolishness of bigotry, the promise of the American dream, and the universal rights of man.

"This fella felt so bad when Barack was finished," Gramps would say, "that he reached into his pocket and gave Barack a hundred dollars on the spot. Paid for all our drinks and food for the rest of the night—and your dad's rent for the rest of the month."

But it was one thing to be Black in Hawaii, a place where

most people's skin was darker than in the rest of the United States. It was another for someone Black to *marry* someone white. In 1960, the year my parents married, more than half the states considered it a felony, a serious crime, for people of different races to have children together. Even in the most sophisticated northern cities, there would be hostile stares and whispers. A white woman pregnant with a Black man's child would probably seriously consider going away until she had the baby and then giving it up for adoption. She might even arrange to end the pregnancy.

It wasn't until 1967—the year I celebrated my sixth birthday, three years after Dr. Martin Luther King, Jr., received the Nobel Peace Prize—that the Supreme Court of the United States would tell the state of Virginia that its ban on interracial marriages violated the U.S. Constitution.

So it is pretty surprising that my grandparents accepted my parents' marriage. I still wonder what about their upbringing made them different from so many other people in those days.

MY GRANDPARENTS WERE raised in Kansas, the center of the country, during the Depression of the 1930s. The people of the state were decent and hardworking. They still had what was called "the pioneer spirit." But side by side with their decency and courage were less worthy qualities. They were suspicious of people who were different, and could be cruel toward them. Many people who didn't play by the rules wound up leaving.

Gramps and Toot grew up less than twenty miles from each other, and they liked to tell stories about small-town life: Fourth of July parades and the movies (or "picture shows") on the side of a barn; fireflies in a jar and the taste of vine-ripe tomatoes, sweet as apples; dust storms and hailstorms and classrooms filled with farm boys who got sewn into their woolen underwear (it had no buttons) at the beginning of winter and stank like pigs as the months wore on. The Depression was full of terrible hardships. Banks lost money and closed down. Poor families lost their farms. But the way my grandparents spoke about that time made it sound like an adventure. Everyone shared the same difficulties, and the experience brought them together.

Gramps and Toot also made sure I knew that there was something called "respectability"—there were respectable people and not-so-respectable people—and although you didn't have to be rich to be respectable, you sure had to work harder at it if you weren't.

Toot's family was respectable. Her grandparents were of Scottish and English stock. Her father held a steady job with a big oil company all through the Depression, and her mother taught school until the children were born. The family kept their house spotless and ordered classic books through the mail. They read the Bible. They chose to be Methodists, which meant they valued calmness and reason. They didn't get as passionate and worked-up as the Baptists, who had big, noisy revival meetings in tents.

Gramps's family was another story. His grandparents had raised him, and they were decent, God-fearing Baptists. But there had been troubles at home. When Gramps was eight, his mother killed herself and he was the one who found her body. People gossiped that his father had been unfaithful and said that was why she'd killed herself.

Whatever the reason, Gramps turned out a bit wild. By the age of fifteen he'd been thrown out of high school for punching the principal in the nose. For the next three years he did odd jobs and jumped freight trains heading for places like Chicago and California. He finally settled in Wichita, Kansas, where Toot's family had moved.

Toot's parents had heard stories about the young man courting their daughter and strongly disapproved of him. The first time Toot brought Gramps over to her house to meet the family, her father took one look at my grandfather's black, slicked-back hair and wise-guy grin and decided he was no good.

My grandmother didn't care. She was fresh out of high school, where she had been a home economics major— which meant learning mostly about cooking, nutrition, and sewing. She was tired of respectability. And my grandfather must have cut a dashing figure. I sometimes imagine them in those years before the war, him in baggy pants and an undershirt, hat cocked back on his head, her a smart-talking girl with too much red lipstick and hair dyed blond and legs nice enough to model stockings for the local department store. He's telling her about the big cities and how he wants to escape from the empty, dust-ridden plains. He says he doesn't want to stay in a place where you know practically on the day that you're born just where you'll die and who it is that'll bury you. He won't end up like that, my grandfather insists; he has dreams, he has plans. She starts to feel as restless for adventure as he does.

They eloped just in time for the Japanese bombing of Pearl Harbor in 1941, and my grandfather joined the army. They never told me much about the war years. I know my mother was born at the army base where Gramps was stationed; that my grandmother, like many women in the 1940s, went to work on a bomber-plane assembly line; and that my grandfather served in France as part of General George S. Patton's army, though he never saw real combat.

When Gramps returned from the war, the family headed to California. He enrolled at the University of California at Berkeley under the GI bill, which made it possible for military veterans like him to study for very little money. But he was too ambitious and restless to stay in school. The family moved back to Kansas, then to a series of small Texas towns, then finally to Seattle, where they bought a house and Gramps worked as a furniture salesman. They were pleased that my mother had turned out to be an excellent student. Even so, when she was offered early admission into the

University of Chicago, my grandfather forbade her to go. He said she was still too young to be living on her own.

And that's where the story might have stopped: a home, a family, a respectable life. Except that my grandfather was always searching for that new start, always running away from the familiar. One day, the manager of the furniture company where he worked happened to mention that a new store was about to open in Honolulu, Hawaii, which at the time was close to becoming the fiftieth state. Gramps rushed home that same day and talked my grandmother into selling their house and packing up yet again, to embark on the final leg of their journey, west, toward the setting sun. . . .

LIKE MANY AMERICAN men of his generation, my grandfather believed in individual liberty. He believed you should have the freedom to do anything you wanted to do and that no one could tell you otherwise. For that time, he was open-minded, and thought of himself as a "free thinker." He wrote poetry on occasion, listened to jazz music, and had close Jewish friends he'd met in the furniture business, even though Christians and Jews didn't always mix then. He enrolled the family in the local Unitarian Universalist church because he liked the idea that Unitarians sometimes borrowed ideas from other religions. "It's like you get five religions in one," he would say. My grandmother was more skeptical by nature. She thought things through for herself and brought Gramps down to earth when his plans weren't realistic.

But in the end, when their daughter declared that she wanted to marry and have a family with a Black man from Kenya, they both remained loyal, supportive, and loving.

And when I was little it seemed that they liked me to know how different they were. Gramps would remind me that Kansas had fought on the Union side of the Civil War, and that some of his relatives had been against slavery. He'd tell me about my great-great-grandfather Christopher Columbus Clark, who had been a decorated Union soldier. And Toot occasionally showed off her beaked nose and jet-black eyes and said she had Cherokee blood in her.

But as I grew older, I found out that wasn't the whole story. Kansas passed a law against slavery, but only after four years of violent battles between pro-slavery forces and anti-slavery "Free-Staters." I learned that another relative on Gramps's side was rumored to have been a second cousin of Jefferson Davis, president of the pro-slavery Confederacy. And I learned that Toot's mother was deeply ashamed that one of her ancestors had been a Native American and had tried to keep it secret.

The truth is that, like most white Americans at the time, my grandparents had never really given Black people much thought. The same unspoken codes that governed life among white people kept personal contact between the races to a minimum; when Black people appear at all in the Kansas of my grandparents' memories, the images are fleeting—Black men who come around the oil fields once in a while, searching for work as hired hands; Black women taking in the white folks' laundry or helping clean white people's homes. Black people are there but not there, like Sam the piano player or Beulah the maid or Amos and Andy on the radio—shadowy, silent presences that elicit neither passion nor fear.

As I began to ask questions about race, I heard stories about its role in their past.

Right after my mother and her parents moved to Texas in the 1950s, Gramps received some friendly advice from his fellow furniture salesmen about serving Black and Mexican customers: "If the coloreds want to look at the merchandise, they need to come after hours and arrange for their own delivery." Later, at the bank where she worked, Toot met the janitor, a tall and dignified Black World War II vet she remembers only as Mr. Reed. While the two of them chatted in the hallway one day, a secretary stormed up and hissed that Toot should never, ever "call no nigger 'Mister.'" Not long afterward, Toot found Mr. Reed in a corner of the building weeping quietly. When she asked him what was wrong, he straightened his back, dried his eyes, and responded with a question of his own.

"What have we ever done to be treated so mean?"

My grandmother didn't have an answer that day, but the question lingered in her mind. Sometimes she and Gramps would discuss it once my mother had gone to bed. According to Toot, the word *racism* wasn't in their vocabulary back then. "Your grandfather and I just figured we should treat people decently, Bar," she told me. "That's all." They decided that Toot would keep calling Mr. Reed "Mister." But the janitor now kept a careful distance when he passed her in the hall. He was afraid for both their sakes. Gramps, meanwhile, was so uncomfortable with racist talk that he began to turn down invitations from his coworkers to go out for a beer, telling them he had to get home. He and Toot began to feel like strangers in their own town.

This unpleasantness in the air hit my mother the hardest. She was eleven or twelve, an only child just growing out of a bad case of asthma. The illness, along with all the moves from town to town, had made her something of a loner—cheerful but prone to bury her head in a book or wander off on walks by herself. My mother made few friends at her new school. She was teased for her name, Stanley Ann (one of Gramps's silly ideas—he had wanted a son). Stanley Steamer, they called her. Stan the Man. When Toot got home from work, she would usually find my mother alone in the front yard, swinging her legs off the porch or lying in the grass, pulled into some lonely world of her own.

Except for that one hot, windless day when Toot came home to find a crowd of children gathered outside the picket fence that surrounded their house. As Toot drew closer, she could make out the sound of mocking laughter, and could see rage and disgust on the children's faces. The children were chanting, in a high-pitched, alternating rhythm:

"Nigger lover!"

"Dirty Yankee!"

"Nigger lover!"

The children scattered when they saw Toot, but not before one of the boys had sent the stone in his hand sailing over the fence. The stone landed at the foot of a tree, and there she saw the cause for all the excitement: my mother and a Black girl of about the same age lying side by side on their stomachs in the grass, their skirts gathered up above their knees, their toes dug into the ground, their heads propped up on their hands in front of one of my mother's books. From a distance the two girls seemed perfectly serene beneath the leafy shade. It was only when Toot opened the gate that she realized the Black girl was shaking and my mother's eyes shone with tears. The girls remained motionless, paralyzed in their fear, until Toot finally leaned down and put her hands on both their heads.

"If you two are going to play," she said, "then for goodness' sake, go on inside. Come on. Both of you." She picked up my mother and reached for the other girl's hand, but before she could say anything more, the girl was in a full sprint, her long legs like a whippet's as she vanished down the street.

Gramps was beside himself when he heard what had happened. He talked to my mother and wrote down the names of all those children. The next day he took the morning off from work to visit the school principal. He personally called the parents of some of the offending children to give them a piece of his mind. And from every adult that he spoke to, he received the same response:

"You best talk to your daughter, Mr. Dunham. White girls don't play with coloreds in this town."

THESE EPISODES WERE not the main reason my grandparents left Texas, but they left their mark. Over the years I have wondered what made my grandfather so angry that day. Maybe because he had grown up without parents in a place where smirks and whispers and gossip had kept him on the outside looking in, he imagined he could understand how the world seemed to people who were Black.

And so, years later, when my mother came home one day and mentioned a friend she had met at the University of Hawaii, an African student named Barack, their first impulse was to invite him over for dinner.

What were they thinking? Gramps might have said, "The poor kid's probably lonely, so far away from home." Toot was cautious and probably wanted to have a look at him. But what did they think when Barack showed up at their door? If I know Gramps, he would have been struck by my father's resemblance to one of his favorite singers, Nat King Cole. Toot would have been polite no matter what she was thinking. When the evening was over, they would both have remarked on how intelligent the young man seemed, so dignified, with that British-sounding accent!

But how did they feel about their daughter marrying a Black man? I don't know how they reacted to the engagement, or what the ceremony was like. There's no record of a real wedding, a cake, a ring, a giving away of the bride. Just a small civil ceremony, performed by a justice of the peace.

My grandparents must have worried, though. In many parts of the South, my father could have been murdered simply for flirting with my mother. Perhaps they held their tongues because they didn't think the marriage would last long.

If so, they underestimated my mother's quiet determination. Pretty soon the baby arrived—eight pounds, two ounces, with ten toes and ten fingers and hungry for food. What in the heck were they supposed to do?

Then the country began to change, and my grandfather had no intention of being left behind. He would listen to his new son-in-law sound off about politics or the economy, about far-off places like the British Parliament or the Kremlin, and imagine a world far different from the one he knew. He read newspapers more carefully, paying special attention to each article about civil rights and racial integration. He believed the world was moving toward Dr. King's magnificent dream.

He began to question how America could be so advanced in its scientific knowledge that it could send men into space and yet so backward in its morals that it kept its Black citizens from having the same opportunities as everyone else. He convinced himself that the world was changing, and that we—our family, not long out of Wichita—were at the forefront of that change. One of my earliest memories is of sitting on my grandfather's shoulders as the astronauts from one of the Apollo missions arrived at Hickam Air Force Base after a splashdown. I remember the astronauts, in aviator glasses, so far away they were barely visible. But Gramps always swore that one of them waved at me—just at me—and that I waved back. It was part of the story he told himself. With his Black son-in-law and his brown grandson, Gramps had entered the space age.

Hawaii, the newest state to join the Union, seemed like the perfect port for setting off on this new adventure. No one seemed to remember that the history of Hawaii was full of injustices. Treaties were signed and broken. Men and women called missionaries who had come from foreign lands to convert the Hawaiians to Christianity accidentally brought diseases that Hawaiians had never known, and those diseases killed many. American companies seized the rich soil to grow sugarcane and pineapple. Japanese, Chinese, and Filipino immigrants earned pennies for working sunup to sunset on plantations. And after Japan attacked the United States during World War II, many Japanese Americans in Hawaii were confined in camps and treated like prisoners. All this was recent history. And yet, by the time my family arrived in 1959, all these injustices seemed to have vanished from people's memories. Now, all of a sudden, Hawaii was hailed as the one true "melting pot," an experiment in racial harmony.

My grandparents threw themselves into that experiment. They wanted to make friends with everyone. My grandfather even had a copy of Dale Carnegie's famous book, *How to Win Friends and Influence People,* which told people how to act to make other people like them—and in some cases to make other people buy things from them. I would hear Gramps talking in a breezy way he must have thought would help him with his customers. He would whip out pictures of the family and offer his life story to strangers; he would pump the hand of the mail carrier or make jokes in bad taste to our waitresses at restaurants.

Sometimes his manners made me cringe, but a lot of people liked that he was so curious, and he made a wide circle of friends. A Japanese American man who ran a small market near our house would save us the choicest cuts of fish for sashimi and give me rice candy with edible wrappers. Every so often, the Hawaiians who worked at my grandfather's store making deliveries would invite us over for roast pig and a native dish called *poi,* which Gramps gobbled down. (My grandmother would wait until she got home and then fix herself some scrambled eggs.)

Sometimes I would accompany Gramps to Ali'i Park, where he liked to play checkers with the old Filipino men who smoked cheap cigars and chewed betel nuts, which had red juice that looked like blood. And I still remember how, one early morning, hours before the sun rose, a Portuguese customer of Gramps's took us out to spear fish off Kailua Bay. A gas lantern hung from the cabin on the small fishing boat as I watched the men dive into inky-black waters, the beams of their flashlights glowing beneath the surface until they emerged with a large fish, iridescent and flopping at the end of one pole. Gramps told me its Hawaiian name, *humu-humu-nuku-nuku-apuaa,* and we repeated it to each other the entire way home.

In such surroundings, my brown skin caused my grandparents few problems, and they got annoyed when visitors made too much of it. Sometimes when Gramps saw tourists watching me play in the sand, he would come up beside them and whisper that I was the great-grandson of King Kamehameha, Hawaii's first king. He was playing a prank on them, of course. But I sometimes wondered if he didn't wish that were the truth. It was so much easier than saying "His mother is white and his father is Black."

There were also times he couldn't resist letting them know how wrong their perceptions were. One day a tourist saw me in the water and was very impressed. "Swimming must just come naturally to these Hawaiian kids," he said. To which Gramps responded that that would be hard to figure, since "that boy happens to be my grandson, his mother is from Kansas, his father is from the interior of Kenya, and there isn't an ocean for miles in either place." For my grandfather, race wasn't something you really needed to worry about anymore. If some people did, well, before long they'd learn not to.

Perhaps my grandfather's journey said as much about the time in which he lived as it did about him. He wanted to be a part of the spirit that, for a fleeting period, gripped the nation. It began with the election of the young, hopeful John F. Kennedy as president of the United States in 1960 and continued through 1965, when Congress passed the Voting Rights Act, which guaranteed the vote to Black people. Many people thought this was the birth of a bright new world without narrow-mindedness and prejudice. Yes, they admitted, there would still be differences. But instead of hating or fearing one another, we'd laugh about those differences and learn from one another's cultures.

The stories my mother and grandparents told about my father were part of this dream of a just world in which all racial barriers would dissolve. That dream cast a spell.

And when that spell was finally broken, when each of them realized it wasn't so easy to escape the worlds they thought they'd left behind, I was still there, occupying the place where their dreams had once been.

CHAPTER 2

One day, when I was six, my mother sat me down to tell me that she was getting married again, and that we would be moving to a faraway place.

She had been dating a man named Lolo since I was four, so I knew him well. He was (as my father had been) a student at the University of Hawaii, and came from a country in Southeast Asia called Indonesia. Lolo's name meant "crazy" in Hawaiian, which always made Gramps laugh. But the meaning didn't suit this Lolo. He had good manners and an easy grace. He was short and brown, handsome, with thick black hair, and he played an excellent tennis game. For the past two years he had endured endless hours of chess with Gramps and long wrestling sessions with me.

I didn't object. I did ask her if she loved Lolo—I had been around long enough to know such things were important. My mother's chin trembled and she looked as though she might cry. She pulled me into a long hug that made me feel very brave, although I wasn't sure why.

Lolo left Hawaii quite suddenly after that, to pick out a house and make other preparations for us in Indonesia, and my mother and I spent much of the next year getting ready for the move. We needed passports, visas, plane tickets, hotel reservations, and an endless series of shots. While we packed, my grandfather pulled out an atlas and showed me where I'd be living. Indonesia is a chain of islands—more than *seventeen thousand* islands, in fact, though only about six thousand are inhabited. Gramps ticked off the names of the more famous ones: Java, Borneo, Sumatra, Bali. When he was my age, they had been called the Spice Islands—enchanted names, shrouded in mystery.

"It says here they still got tigers over there," he said. "And orangutangs." He looked up from the book and his eyes widened. "Says here they even got *headhunters!*"

The country's government had recently been overthrown by a new group of officials, but news reports in the United States said there had been little violence. Toot called the State Department to find out if the country was stable and was told that the situation was "under control." Still, she insisted that we pack several trunks full of food in case of emergency: Tang, powdered milk, cans of sardines. "You never know what these people will eat," she said firmly. My mother sighed, but Toot tossed in several boxes of candy to win me over to her side.

My mother warned me that Indonesia was a very

poor country. She said there was a chance we could get dysentery—a bacterial infection that causes severe diarrhea—and that I might have to get used to cold-water baths and days when the lights would go out. But these were only small inconveniences, she insisted. I could tell she was excited by the promise of something new and important. She thought that she and her new husband could help rebuild the country. Also, it would be good finally to get away from her parents, even though she loved them.

At last, we boarded a jet for our flight around the globe. I wore a long-sleeved white shirt and a gray clip-on tie, and the stewardesses gave me puzzles and extra peanuts and a set of metal pilot's wings. As we walked off the plane in the country's capital city, Jakarta, the sun seemed as hot as a furnace. I clutched my mother's hand. I was determined to protect her from whatever might come.

Lolo was there to greet us, a few pounds heavier and with a bushy mustache. He hugged my mother, hoisted me up into the air, and told us to follow a small, wiry man who was carrying our luggage straight past the long line at customs and into a waiting car. My mother said something to the man and he laughed and nodded, but it was clear he didn't understand a word of English. People swirled around us, speaking rapidly in a language I didn't know, smelling unfamiliar.

The car was borrowed, Lolo told us, but he had bought a brand-new motorcycle. The new house was finished, with only a few touch-ups left to be done. I was already enrolled in a nearby school, and Lolo's parents and cousins and friends were excited to meet us. As he and my mother talked, I stuck my head out the back window and stared at the brown and green landscape and smelled diesel oil and wood smoke. Men and women stepped like cranes through rice paddies, their faces hidden by their straw hats. A boy, wet and slick as an otter, sat on the back of a water buffalo, whipping its haunch with a stick of bamboo. Then the streets became more congested. Small stores appeared, along with men pulling carts loaded with stone and timber. The buildings began to grow taller, like the ones in Hawaii.

"There's the Hotel Indonesia," said Lolo. "Very modern. There's the new shopping center." But only a few of the buildings were higher than the trees that now cooled the road.

When we passed a row of big houses with high hedges and guards, my mother said something I didn't understand about the government and a man named Sukarno.

"Who's Sukarno?" I shouted from the backseat, but Lolo appeared not to hear me. Instead, he touched my arm and motioned ahead of us. "Look," he said, pointing upward. There beside the road was a towering giant at least ten stories tall, with the body of a man and the face of an ape. It was a statue.

"That's Hanuman, the monkey god," Lolo said.

I was amazed by the solitary figure, so dark against the sun. It looked as if it were about to leap into the sky as puny cars swirled around its feet. "He's a great warrior," Lolo said. "Strong as a hundred men. When he fights the demons, he's never defeated."

Our house was on the outskirts of town. The road ran over a narrow bridge over a wide brown river; and as we passed, I could see villagers bathing and washing clothes along the steep banks below. The road turned to gravel and then to dirt as it wound past small stores and whitewashed bungalows until it finally petered out into the narrow footpaths of the *kampong,* or compound. The house itself was modest stucco and red tile, but it was open and airy, with a big mango tree in the small courtyard in front.

As we passed through the gate, Lolo announced that he had a surprise for me; but before he could explain we heard a deafening howl from high up in the tree. My mother and I jumped back and saw a big, hairy creature with a small, flat head and long, menacing arms drop onto a low branch.

"A monkey!" I shouted.

"An ape," my mother corrected me.

Lolo drew a peanut from his pocket and handed it to the animal's grasping fingers. "His name is Tata," he said. "I brought him all the way from New Guinea for you."

I started to step forward to get a closer look, but Tata threatened to lunge, his dark-ringed eyes fierce and suspicious. I decided to stay where I was.

"Don't worry," Lolo said, handing Tata another peanut. "He's on a leash. Come—there's more."

I looked up at my mother, and she gave me a tentative smile. In the backyard, we found what seemed like a small zoo: chickens and ducks running every which way, a big yellow dog with a scary howl, two birds of paradise, a white cockatoo, and two baby crocodiles, half underwater in a fenced-off pond. Lolo stared down at the reptiles.

"There were three," he said, "but the biggest one crawled out through a hole in the fence. Slipped into somebody's rice field and ate one of the man's ducks. We had to hunt it by torchlight."

There wasn't much light left, but we took a short walk down the mud path into the village. Groups of giggling neighborhood children waved from their compounds, and a few barefoot old men came up to shake our hands. We stopped at the town center, the "common," where a man Lolo knew was grazing a few goats, and a small boy came up beside me, holding a dragonfly that hovered at the end of a string.

When we returned to the house, the man who had carried our luggage was standing in the backyard with a rust-colored hen tucked under his arm and a long knife in his right hand. He said something to Lolo, who nodded and called over to my mother and me. My mother told me to wait where I was and looked questioningly at Lolo.

"Don't you think he's a little young?" she asked him.

Lolo shrugged and looked down at me. "The boy should know where his dinner is coming from. What do you think, Barry?"

I looked at my mother, then turned back to face the man holding the chicken. Lolo nodded again, and I watched the man set the bird down, pinning it gently under one knee and pulling its neck out across a narrow gutter. For a moment the bird struggled, beating its wings hard against the ground, a few feathers dancing up with the wind. Then it grew completely still. The man pulled the blade across the bird's neck in a single smooth motion. Blood shot out in a long, crimson ribbon. The man stood up, holding the bird far away from his body, and suddenly tossed it high into the air. It landed with a thud, then struggled to its feet, its legs pumping wildly in a wide, wobbly circle. I watched as the circle grew smaller, until finally the bird collapsed, lifeless on the grass.

Lolo rubbed his hand across my head and told me and my mother to go wash up before dinner. The three of us ate quietly under a dim yellow bulb—chicken stew and rice, and then a dessert of red, hairy-skinned fruit so sweet at the center that only a stomachache could make me stop eating. Later, lying alone beneath a mosquito net canopy, I listened to the crickets chirp under the moonlight and remembered the chicken's last twitch of life. I could hardly believe my good fortune.

ONE DAY NOT long after my arrival in Indonesia, I was playing soccer with a friend and in the middle of the game an older boy jumped in and ran off with the ball. I chased after him, but when I got close he picked up a rock and threw it at me. By the time I got home I had an egg-sized lump on the side of my head. When Lolo saw me, he looked up from washing his motorcycle and asked what had happened. I told him the story.

"It's not fair," I said, my voice choking. "He cheated."

Lolo parted my hair with his fingers to examine the wound. "It's not bleeding," he said finally. Then he went back to his motorcycle.

I thought that was the end of it. But when he came home from work the next day, he had two pairs of boxing gloves. They smelled of new leather. The larger pair was black, the smaller pair red. I put on the red pair and he tied the laces, then stepped back to inspect me. My hands dangled at my sides like bulbs at the ends of thin stalks. He shook his head and raised the gloves to cover my face. We faced off in the backyard.

"The first thing to remember is how to protect yourself. There. Keep your hands up." He adjusted my elbows, then crouched into a stance and started to bob. "You want to keep moving, but always stay low—don't give them a target. How does that feel?"

I nodded, copying his movements as best I could. After a few minutes, he stopped and held his palm up in front of my nose.

"Okay," he said. "Let's see your swing."

This I could do. I took a step back, wound up, and delivered my best shot into his hand. It barely wobbled.

"Not bad," Lolo said. He nodded, his expression unchanged. "Not bad at all. Agh, but look where your hands are now. What did I tell you? Get them up. . . ."

I raised my arms, throwing soft jabs at Lolo's palm, glancing up at him every so often and realizing how familiar his face had become after our two years together, as familiar as the earth on which we stood.

IT HAD TAKEN me less than six months to learn Indonesia's language, its customs, and its legends. I had survived chicken pox, measles, and the sting of my teachers' bamboo switches. The children of farmers, servants, and low-level government workers had become my best friends, and together we ran the streets morning and night, hustling odd jobs and catching crickets. One of our games was to try to cut the lines of one another's kites: The loser would watch his soar off with the wind while other children would chase after it, waiting for their prize to land. With Lolo, I learned how to eat small green chili peppers raw with dinner (plenty of rice), and, away from the dinner table, I was introduced to dog meat (tough), snake meat (tougher), and roasted grasshopper (crunchy). Like many Indonesians, Lolo followed a brand of the Islamic religion that included elements from other faiths. Like the Hindus, he believed that a man took on the powers of whatever he ate. One day soon, he promised, he would bring home a piece of tiger meat for us to share.

That's how things were, one long adventure. My grandparents sent packages of chocolate and peanut butter, and I wrote to them faithfully. But some things about this strange new land I found too difficult to explain.

I didn't tell Toot and Gramps about the man who had come to our door one day with a gaping hole where his nose should have been, and the whistling sound he made as he asked my mother for food.

I didn't mention the story that one of my friends had told me, about the wind that had brought an evil spirit the night before and killed his baby brother. He wasn't trying to frighten me. There was terror in his eyes.

I didn't write about the look on the faces of farmers when the rains didn't come, about the stoop in their shoulders as they wandered barefoot through their barren, cracked fields. I didn't write about how desperate those same farmers were when the rains lasted for over a month and the river overflowed and the streets gushed with water, as high as my waist. I didn't write about the families who scrambled to rescue their goats and hens as chunks of their huts washed away.

The world was violent, I was learning, unpredictable and often cruel. My grandparents knew nothing about such a world, I decided, so there was no point in bothering them with questions they couldn't answer. Sometimes, when my mother came home from her job at the U.S. Embassy, I would tell her the things I had seen or heard, and she would stroke my forehead and try her best to explain what she could. I liked the attention—her voice, the touch of her hand, made me feel secure. But she didn't know anything more about floods and evil winds than I did. I would go away feeling that my questions had only worried her unnecessarily.

So I would turn to Lolo for guidance. He didn't talk much, but he was easy to be with. With his family and friends he introduced me as his son, but he never pretended to be my real father. Somehow this didn't bother me. I liked that he treated me more like a man than a child. And his knowledge of the world seemed inexhaustible. Not just how to change a flat tire or make the opening move in a chess game. He knew ways to help me manage my emotions. He knew how to explain the mysteries that surrounded me.

Like how to deal with beggars. They seemed to be every-where—men, women, children, in tattered clothing matted with dirt, some without arms, others without feet, victims of untreated diseases like polio or leprosy, walking on their hands or rolling down the crowded sidewalks in homemade carts. At first, I watched my mother give her money to anyone who stopped at our door or stretched out an arm as we passed on the streets. Later, when it became clear that the tide of pain was endless, she gave to fewer people, doing her best to figure out who needed her help the most. Lolo was touched by her calculations but thought they were silly. Whenever he caught me following her example and giving away the few coins I had, he would take me aside.

"How much money do you have?" he would ask.

I'd empty my pocket. "Thirty rupiah."

"How many beggars are there on the street?"

I tried to imagine the number that had come by the house in the last week. "You see?" he said, once it was clear I'd lost count. "Better to save your money and make sure you don't end up on the street yourself."

He was the same way about servants. They were mostly young people who had just arrived in the big city from small villages. Often they worked for families that didn't have much more money than they did. They would send the small amount they earned to their families back home, or try to save enough to start their own businesses. If they were hard workers, Lolo was willing to help them. But he would fire them without a second thought if they were clumsy or forgetful, or cost him money. And he was baffled when either my mother or I defended them.

"Your mother has a soft heart," Lolo told me one day, after my mother tried to take the blame for knocking a radio off the dresser. "That's a good thing in a woman. But you will be a man someday, and a man needs to have more sense."

It had nothing to do with good or bad, he explained, like or dislike. It was a matter of taking life on its own terms.

I FELT A hard knock to the jaw. Lolo wanted to spar with me.

"Pay attention. Keep your hands up."

We threw punches for another half hour before Lolo decided it was time for a rest. My arms burned; my head flashed with a dull, steady throb. We took a jug full of water and sat down near the crocodile pond.

"Tired?" he asked me.

I slumped forward, barely nodding. He smiled, and rolled up one of his pant legs to scratch his calf. I noticed a series of scars that ran from his ankle halfway up his shin.

"What are those?"

"Leech marks," he said. "From when I was in New Guinea. They crawl inside your army boots while you're hiking through the swamps. At night, when you take off your socks, they're stuck there, fat with blood. You sprinkle salt on them and they die, but you still have to dig them out with a hot knife."

I ran my finger over one of the oval grooves. It was smooth and hairless where the skin had been singed. I asked Lolo if it had hurt.

"Of course it hurt," he said, taking a sip from the jug. "Sometimes you can't worry about hurt. Sometimes you worry only about getting where you have to go."

We fell silent, and I watched him out of the corner of my eye. I realized that I had never heard him talk about what he was feeling. I had never seen him really angry or sad. A strange notion suddenly sprang into my head.

"Have you ever seen a man killed?" I asked him.

He glanced down, surprised by the question.

"Have you?" I asked again.

"Yes," he said.

"Was it bloody?"

"Yes."

I thought for a moment. "Why was the man killed? The one you saw?"

"Because he was weak."

"That's all?"

Lolo shrugged and rolled his pant leg back down. "That's usually enough. Men take advantage of weakness in other men. They're just like countries in that way. The strong man takes the weak man's land. He makes the weak man work in his fields. If the weak man's woman is pretty, the strong man will take her." He paused to take another sip of water, then asked, "Which would you rather be?"

I didn't answer, and Lolo squinted up at the sky. "Better to be strong," he said finally, rising to his feet. "If you can't be strong, be clever and make peace with someone who's strong. But always better to be strong yourself. Always."

MY MOTHER HAD expected this new life to be difficult. Before leaving Hawaii, she had tried to learn all she could about Indonesia. She learned that it was the country with the fifth largest population in the world, with hundreds of ethnic groups and dialects. She learned that it had long been under the control of other countries greedy for its vast amounts of oil and timber. The Dutch ruled Indonesia for over three centuries, and the Japanese took over during World War II. She learned about Indonesia's battle for independence. A freedom fighter named Sukarno became the country's first president but had just been replaced. Some said he was corrupt. Others said he was too comfortable with the Communists.

It was a poor country, different from the one she had known, and my mother was prepared for its hardships. She was prepared to squat over a hole in the ground to pee. She was prepared for the heat and mosquitoes. What she wasn't prepared for was the loneliness. It was constant, like a shortness of breath. There was nothing definite that she could point to, really. Lolo was kind and had gone out of his way to make her feel at home, and his family was generous to her.

But something had happened between her and Lolo in the year that they had been apart. In Hawaii he had been so full of life, so eager with his plans. At night when they were alone, he would tell her about growing up as a boy during the war, watching his father and eldest brother leave to join the revolutionary army, hearing the news that both had been killed and everything lost. He would tell her how the Dutch army had set his family's house on fire, how they'd fled to the countryside, how his mother had been forced to sell her gold jewelry one piece at a time in exchange for food. He told her that now that the Dutch had been driven out of the country, everything would change. He intended to return and teach at the university and be a part of that change.

He didn't talk that way anymore. In fact, he barely spoke to her at all, unless it was about repairing a leak or planning a trip to visit some distant cousin. It was as if he had pulled into some dark hidden place, taking with him the brightest part of himself. On some nights, she would hear him up after everyone else had gone to bed, wandering through the house, drinking whiskey from a bottle. Other nights he would tuck a pistol under his pillow before falling off to sleep. Whenever she asked him what was wrong, he would say he was just tired.

She suspected these problems had to do with Lolo's job. He was working for the army as a geologist, surveying roads and tunnels. It was mind-numbing work that didn't pay much. Our refrigerator alone cost two months' salary. And now he had a wife and child to support . . . no wonder he was depressed. My mother hadn't traveled all this way to be a burden, she decided. She would earn money, too.

She found a job right away teaching English to Indonesian businessmen at the American embassy. The money helped, but she was still terribly lonely. The Americans at the embassy were mostly older men and made rude jokes about Indonesians until they found out that she was married to one. Still, over lunch or in casual conversation these men told her things about Indonesia that she couldn't learn in the newspapers. They explained that the U.S. government had been upset by Sukarno's Communist leanings and had decided he wasn't a friend to America. Word was that the U.S.

Central Intelligence Agency (the CIA) had played a part in the military operation that brought him to power, although at the time nobody knew for sure. After the takeover, they told her, the military had swept the countryside and killed anyone thought to be a Communist sympathizer. The death toll was anybody's guess: a few hundred thousand, maybe; half a million.

It came as a shock to my mother to find out that we had arrived in Jakarta less than a year after this wave of brutal killings. It was frightening that history could be swallowed up so completely, that people continued to go about their business beneath giant posters of the new president as if nothing had happened. As her circle of Indonesian friends widened, a few of them whispered other stories—about the corruption throughout the new government, the bribes demanded by police and the military, and the crooked business activities of the president's family and friends. With each new story, she would go to Lolo in private and ask: "Is it true?"

He would never answer. "Why are you worrying about such talk?" he would ask her. "Why don't you buy a new dress?"

She finally complained to one of Lolo's cousins, a pediatrician who had helped look after Lolo during the war.

"You don't understand," the cousin told her gently.

"Understand what?"

"Lolo didn't plan on coming back from Hawaii so early.

During the military takeover, all students studying abroad were told to return immediately, with no explanation, and their passports were taken away. So when Lolo stepped off the plane, he had no idea what would happen next. The army officials took him away and questioned him. They told him that he had just been conscripted and would be going to the jungles of New Guinea for a year. And he was one of the lucky ones. Some of the students who were told to come back are still in jail. Or they vanished.

"You shouldn't be too hard on Lolo," the cousin said. "Such times are best forgotten."

My mother left the cousin's house in a daze. Outside, the sun was high, the air full of dust, but instead of taking a taxi home, she began to walk without direction.

She could not stop thinking about the word *power*. In America, power was generally hidden from view. Everyone was supposed to be equal, and that's what you believed—unless you visited an American Indian reservation or spoke to a Black person who trusted you. Then you saw clearly what was hidden under the surface. But in Indonesia, power was not disguised. People who had it were open about it. People who didn't, like Lolo, knew their lives were not their own. That's how things were; you couldn't change it, you could just live by the rules, so simple once you learned them. And so Lolo had made his peace with power. He learned to forget he had no freedom. His brother-in-law had also "forgotten" and had managed to become successful, making a fortune as a high official in the national oil company. Another brother, though, had made mistakes. He would steal silverware whenever he came for a visit. Lolo understood that in this country, a man like him could make one slip and tumble backward.

My mother was a foreigner, middle-class and white. She could always leave if things got too messy. The difference in their positions created a gap between her and Lolo that could never be bridged.

I'm not sure Lolo ever fully understood what my mother was going through, why the things he was working so hard to provide for her seemed only to increase the distance between them. He was not a man to ask himself such questions. Instead, he concentrated on rising in society. With the help of his brother-in-law, he landed a new job in the government relations office of an American oil company. We moved to a house in a better neighborhood; a car replaced the motorcycle; a television and hi-fi replaced the crocodiles and Tata, the ape. Sometimes I would overhear him and my mother arguing in their bedroom, usually when she refused to attend his company dinner parties, where white American businessmen from Texas and Louisiana would slap Lolo's back and boast about the bribes they had paid for offshore oil drilling rights, while their wives complained to my mother about the incompetence of Indonesian housekeepers. Lolo would tell her it looked bad for him to go alone and remind her that these were her own people, and my mother's voice would rise to almost a shout.

"They are *not* my people," she would say.

Such arguments were rare, though. My mother and Lolo remained on good terms through the birth of my sister, Maya, and through their separation and eventual divorce. Ten years later, when I was in my teens, my mother even helped Lolo travel to Los Angeles to treat the liver disease that would kill him. It was the last time I saw him.

It turned out that the tension I noticed had mainly to do with me. My mother had always encouraged me to adapt to Indonesia, and I had. I took care of myself, I didn't complain about not having much money, and I was extremely well mannered compared to other American children. Too often Americans abroad didn't learn about the places they visited and acted high and mighty, and she taught me never to be that way. But she had finally realized that I would have many more opportunities in America than in Indonesia, and that my true life lay elsewhere.

THE FIRST STEP was to make sure I got a good education. Since my mother and Lolo didn't have the money to send me to the International School, where most of Jakarta's foreign children went, my mother arranged to add to my Indonesian schooling with lessons from a U.S. correspondence course—lessons that came in the mail. Five days a week, she appeared in my room at four in the morning, force-fed me breakfast, and taught me English lessons for three hours before I left for school and she went to work. I resisted. I'd tell her my stomach hurt. Sometimes my eyes kept closing every five minutes. But she was determined, and she would patiently say:

"This is no picnic for me either, buster."

It wasn't just my education my mother was worried about. The longer we stayed, the more concerned she grew about my safety.

One night, a friend and I hitchhiked out to his family's farm. It started to rain, and there was a terrific place to mudslide. But at the bottom of the hill there was this barbed-wire fence. . . .

I got home after dark and found a large search party of neighbors in our yard. My mother didn't look happy, but she was so relieved to see me that it took her several minutes to notice the wet sock, brown with mud, wrapped around my forearm.

"What's that?"

"What?"

"That. Why do you have a sock wrapped around your arm?"

"I cut myself."

"Let's see."

"It's not that bad."

"*Barry*. Let me see it."

I unwrapped the sock, exposing a long gash that ran from my wrist to my elbow. It had missed the vein by an inch, but ran deeper at the muscle, where pinkish flesh pulsed out from under the skin.

She was not happy when Lolo suggested we wait until morning to get me stitched up. She badgered our only neighbor with a car into driving us to the hospital. Most of the lights were out when we arrived, with no receptionist in sight and only the sound of my mother's frantic footsteps echoing through the hallway. Finally she found two young men in boxer shorts playing dominoes in a small room in the back. When she asked them where the doctors were, the men cheerfully replied, "We are the doctors," and went on to finish their game before getting dressed and giving me twenty stitches that would leave an ugly scar.

Years later she told me that she had had the feeling that my life might slip away when she wasn't looking, that everyone else around her would be too busy trying to survive to notice.

But there was something even more important to her than school transcripts or medical services, and that became the focus of her lessons with me. She was afraid that I would take the wrong lessons from Indonesia and wanted to teach me the virtues she had learned in her Midwestern childhood. "If you want to grow into a human being," she would say, "you're going to need some values."

She made her points using examples from our lives:

Honesty—Do not imitate Lolo, who hides the refrigerator in the storage room when the officials come so he doesn't have to pay taxes on it. In Indonesia, even the tax officials expect such behavior, but it isn't right, here or anywhere.

Fairness—The parents of the richer students should not

give television sets to the teachers in the hope of getting their children higher grades. If those children do receive better marks, they should take no pride in them.

Straight talk—If you didn't like the shirt I bought you for your birthday, you should have just said so instead of keeping it wadded up at the bottom of your closet.

Independent judgment—Just because the other children tease the poor boy about his haircut doesn't mean you have to do it too.

Unfortunately, there was not much that reinforced her lessons. I would nod dutifully, but I thought her ideas were impractical. All around me I saw poverty, corruption, cynicism, and people who would do anything for a little security. They lived hard lives and seemed to accept their fate. I didn't have her faith in the goodness of people and their ability to shape their own destinies. It was only much later that I appreciated the power of her humanism, which I came to see as part of a larger tradition in the United States— the values that gave America such things as Franklin Delano Roosevelt's New Deal and the Peace Corps.

The most persuasive example she could offer was, strangely enough, my distant father. She would remind me of his story, how he had grown up poor, in a poor country, on a poor continent; how his life had been hard, as hard as anything that Lolo might have known. He hadn't cut corners, though, or played all the angles. He was hardworking and honest, no matter what it cost him. He had led his life according to principles that demanded a different kind of toughness, principles that would lead to a higher form of power. I would follow his example, my mother decided. I had no choice, she told me. It was in my genes.

My mother set out to teach me about the Black experience in America. She would come home with books on the civil rights movement, the recordings of gospel singer Mahalia Jackson, the speeches of Dr. King. When she told me stories of schoolchildren in the South who had to read hand-me-down books from rich white schools but went on to become doctors and lawyers and scientists, I felt ashamed of my reluctance to wake up and study in the mornings. According to her, every Black man could be the great Supreme Court justice Thurgood Marshall or the actor Sidney Poitier; every Black woman could be the voting rights leader Fannie Lou Hamer or the magnificent jazz singer Lena Horne. To be Black was to inherit a special destiny. There were burdens, but we and only we were strong enough to bear them. And we were meant to carry those burdens with style. More than once, my mother told me the calypso singer Harry Belafonte was "the best-looking man on the planet."

But I learned that not every Black person was able to appreciate that heritage. One day my mother took me to the American embassy, where I sat in the library while she went off to do some work. After I had finished my comic books and my homework, I found a collection of American magazines neatly displayed in clear plastic binders. In one of them I came across a photograph of an older man in dark glasses and a raincoat walking down an empty road. On the next page was another photograph, this one a close-up of the same man's hands. They were strangely, unnaturally pale, as if blood had been drawn from his flesh. Turning back to the first picture, I now saw that the man's crinkly hair, his heavy lips and broad, fleshy nose, all had this same uneven, ghostly hue.

I thought maybe he had been poisoned by radiation, or maybe he was an albino—I had seen one of them on the street and my mother had explained about such things. Except when I read the words that went with the picture, that wasn't it at all. The man had received a chemical treatment, the article explained, to lighten his complexion, so he could pass for a white man. He had paid for it with his own money. He was full of regret. Things had turned out badly; the results were irreversible.

It turned out there were thousands of people like him, Black folks back in America who'd undergone the same treatment in response to advertisements that promised them happiness as a white person.

I felt my face and neck get hot. My stomach knotted; the type began to blur on the page. Did my mother know about this? I had a desperate urge to jump out of my seat, to demand some explanation or reassurance. But something held me back. As in a bad dream, I had no voice to tell my mother what I was feeling. By the time she came to take me home, my face wore a smile and the magazines were back in their proper place.

But I never got over the shock of that revelation. I still think about Black children who have had similar moments— the young boy who is warned by his parents not to cross the boundary of a particular neighborhood, or the young girl frustrated at not having hair like Barbie, no matter how long she teases and combs. Maybe a father or grandfather tells them a story of being humiliated by an employer or a police officer. When I imagine those small doses of bad news, week after week, I suspect I was lucky to grow up the way that I did. I had a long stretch of childhood free of such self-doubt.

My mother warned me about bigots, of course. She said they were ignorant, uneducated people who I should avoid. But that one photograph had told me something else: that there was a hidden enemy out there, one that could reach me without my even knowing. When I got home that night from the embassy library, I went into the bathroom and stood in front of the mirror looking at myself and wondering if there was something wrong with me.

My anxiety passed, and I spent my final year in Indonesia much as I had before, confident and often mischievous. But my vision had been permanently altered. On the imported television shows that had started running in the evenings, I began to notice that the Black man on *Mission: Impossible* spent all his time underground. I noticed that there was nobody like me in the department store Christmas catalogs that Toot and Gramps sent us, and that Santa was a white man.

I kept these observations to myself, deciding that either my mother didn't see them or she was trying to protect me. I still trusted her love—but I now faced the possibility that her account of the world, and my father's place in it, was somehow incomplete.

CHAPTER 3

When I had finished all the lessons of my correspondence course, my mother said it was time for me to go back to Hawaii, live with my grandparents, and attend an American school. The new arrangement didn't sound so bad when she first explained it to me. She said that she and my sister Maya would be joining me in Hawaii very soon—a year, tops. She reminded me what a great time I'd had living with Gramps and Toot the previous summer—the ice cream, the cartoons, the days at the beach. "And you won't have to wake up at four in the morning," she said. That would be the best part.

But when I landed in Honolulu, I felt more uncertain. It took me a while to recognize Gramps and Toot in the blur of smiling, anxious faces. Eventually I spotted a tall, silver-haired man at the back of the crowd, with a short, owlish woman barely visible beside him. I was carrying a wooden mask, a gift from the Indonesian copilot, a friend of my mother's who had taken me to the plane as she and Lolo waved goodbye. The wood had a nutty, cinnamon smell, and as I inhaled it I felt myself drifting back across oceans and over clouds, back to the place where I had been. Without thinking, I brought the mask up to my face and swayed my head in an odd little dance. My grandparents laughed.

Just then a customs official tapped me on the shoulder and asked if I was an American. I nodded and handed him my passport. "Go ahead," he said, telling the Chinese family in line ahead of me to step to one side. I remembered how lively they'd been on the plane, but as I passed them they stood absolutely still, and I saw hands rifling through their passports and luggage.

Toot gathered me into a hug and tossed candy-and-chewing-gum Hawaiian leis around my neck. Gramps threw an arm over my shoulder and joked that the mask was a definite improvement over my face. They took me to their new car, and Gramps showed me how to operate the air-conditioning. We drove along the highway, past fast-food restaurants and cheap motels and used-car lots. I told them about the trip and everyone back in Jakarta. Gramps told me what they'd planned for my welcome-back dinner. Toot looked at what I was wearing and said, gently, that I'd need new clothes for school.

Then, suddenly, the conversation stopped. And I realized all at once that I was going to live with strangers.

The two of them had changed. After my mother and I left for Indonesia, they had sold the big, rambling house near the university and rented a small, two-bedroom apartment in a high-rise building. Gramps had left the furniture business to become a life insurance agent, but since he was unable to convince himself that people needed what he was selling and was hurt by rejection, the work went badly. Every Sunday night, I watched him grow more and more irritable as it came time to chase us out of the living room and try to schedule appointments with potential clients over the phone.

Sometimes I would tiptoe into the kitchen for a soda and hear the desperation in his voice, the silence that followed when the people he was talking to said, no, Thursday wasn't good and Tuesday not much better. Gramps would fumble through the files in his lap and sigh heavily after he hung up the phone.

Eventually, though, he'd convince a few people to meet with him, his pain would pass, and Gramps would wander into my room to tell me stories of his youth or the new joke he had read in *Reader's Digest*. If his phone calls had gone especially well, he might discuss with me some scheme he still harbored—the book of poems he had started to write, the sketch he intended to turn into a painting, the floor plans for his ideal house. The bolder his plans, the less likely they seemed, but I recognized some of his old enthusiasm, and I tried to think up encouraging questions to keep up his good mood. Then, somewhere in the middle of his presentation, we would both notice Toot standing in the hall outside my room.

"What do you want, Madelyn?"

"Are you finished with your calls, dear?"

"*Yes, Madelyn.* I'm finished with my calls. It's ten o'clock at night!"

"There's no need to holler, Stanley. I just wanted to know if I could go into the kitchen."

"I'm not hollering!"

Toot would retreat into their bedroom, and Gramps would leave my room with a look of dejection and rage.

What was all that about? Scenes like that became familiar to me, and I soon realized the tension had something to do with the rarely mentioned fact that Toot was earning more money than Gramps. In those days wives almost never made more than their husbands, but Toot was a trailblazer. She had become the first woman vice president of a local bank, and although Gramps liked to say that he always encouraged her in her career, he couldn't help but be ashamed that he paid fewer and fewer of the family's bills.

Toot hadn't expected to be so successful. She had no college education, and she had only become a secretary after I was born, to help my mother financially. But she had a quick mind, good judgment, and the capacity for hard work. Slowly she had risen, playing by the rules—until, as a woman, she couldn't rise any higher. It didn't matter how competent she was. For twenty years she watched her male colleagues move up past her, becoming wealthy men.

More than once, my mother would tell Toot that the bank shouldn't get away with such obvious sexism—promoting men over women who were more qualified. But Toot would just pooh-pooh my mother's remarks, saying that everybody could find a reason to complain about something. Toot didn't complain. Every morning, she woke up at five a.m., powdered her face, and put on a tailored suit and high-heeled pumps. Then she would board the six-thirty bus to arrive at her downtown office before anyone else. She took pride in her work. She liked to read an article about money in the newspaper and be able to tell us the inside story, the real story.

When I got older, though, she would confide in me that she had never stopped dreaming of a different kind of life: a house with a white picket fence, days spent baking or playing bridge or volunteering at the local library. I was surprised, because she rarely mentioned hopes or regrets. And I don't know if she would *really* have preferred that other life, the life of a woman who didn't have to work. But when I was older I came to understand that at the time she built her career, a wife working outside the home was nothing to brag about, for her or for Gramps. She did it for me.

"So long as you kids do well, Bar," she would say more than once, "that's all that really matters."

They hardly had people over to dinner anymore. We didn't go to the beach or on hikes together. At night, Gramps watched television while Toot sat in her room reading murder mysteries. They should have been enjoying the middle years of their lives, a time when people can begin to feel satisfied with their accomplishments and still have plenty of time left to look forward to. But they were just hanging on, going through the motions. At some point while I was in Indonesia, they had given up the dreams that had brought them to Hawaii. They saw no more destinations to hope for.

THERE WAS ONE thing that filled my grandparents with pride: I had gotten into the prestigious Punahou Academy. Founded by missionaries in 1841, Punahou was now the school of choice for the children of Hawaii's rich and powerful. It hadn't been easy to get in; there was a long waiting list. But the school agreed to consider me after they were contacted by Gramps's boss, who had gone there years before. So my first experience with "affirmative action" had little to do with race and a lot to do with who my family knew.

When I applied, Gramps and I took a tour of the campus, and we were amazed by the acres of lush green fields and shady trees, the old masonry schoolhouses and modern structures of glass and steel. There were tennis courts, swimming pools, and photography studios. At one point, Gramps grabbed me by the arm. "This isn't a school," he whispered. "This is heaven. You might just get me to go back to school with you."

With my acceptance came a thick packet of information. "Welcome to the Punahou family," the letter announced. A locker had been assigned to me; I was enrolled in a meal plan; and there was a list of things to buy—a uniform for physical education, scissors, a ruler, number two pencils, a calculator (optional). Gramps spent the evening reading the entire school catalog, everything that would be expected from me over the next seven years. With each new item, Gramps grew more and more excited; several times he got up, with his thumb saving his place, and headed toward the room where Toot was reading, his voice full of amazement: "Madelyn, get a load of this!"

So Gramps was thrilled to take me to my first day of school. He insisted that we arrive early, and Castle Hall, the building for the fifth and sixth graders, was not yet open. We sat beside a slender Chinese boy who had a large dental retainer strapped around his neck.

"Hi there," Gramps said to the boy. "This here's Barry. I'm Barry's grandfather. You can call me Gramps." He shook hands with the boy, whose name was Frederick. "Barry's new."

"Me too," Frederick said, and the two of them launched into a lively conversation. I sat, embarrassed, until the doors finally opened and we went up the stairs to our classroom. At the door, Gramps slapped both of us on the back.

"Don't do anything I would do," he said with a grin.

"Your grandfather's funny," Frederick said as we watched Gramps introduce himself to Miss Hefty, our homeroom teacher.

"Yeah. He is."

We sat at a table with four other children, and Miss Hefty, an energetic middle-aged woman with short gray hair, took attendance. When she read my full name—Barack Hussein Obama— I heard snickering. Frederick leaned over to me.

"I thought your name was Barry."

"Would you prefer if we called you Barry?" Miss Hefty asked. "Barack is such a beautiful name. Your grandfather tells me your father is Kenyan. I used to live in Kenya, you know. Teaching children just your age. It's such a magnificent country. Do you know what tribe your father is from?"

Her question brought on more giggles, and I remained speechless for a moment. When I finally said "Luo," a sandy-haired boy behind me repeated the word in a loud hoot, like the sound of a monkey. The children could no longer contain themselves, and it took a stern reprimand from Miss Hefty before the class would settle down and we could mercifully move on to the next person on the list.

I spent the rest of the day in a daze. A redheaded girl asked to touch my hair and seemed hurt when I refused. A ruddy-faced boy asked me if my father ate people. When I got home, Gramps was in the middle of preparing dinner.

"So how was it? Isn't it terrific that Miss Hefty used to live in Kenya? Makes the first day a little easier, I'll bet."

I went into my room and closed the door.

The novelty of having me in the class quickly wore off for the other kids, but my sense that I didn't belong continued to grow. The clothes that Gramps and I had chosen for me were too old-fashioned; the Indonesian sandals that had been just fine in Jakarta seemed dowdy. Most of my classmates had been together since kindergarten; they lived in the same neighborhoods, in split-level homes with swimming pools; their fathers coached the same Little League teams; their mothers sponsored the bake sales. Nobody played soccer or badminton or chess like the kids in Jakarta, and I had no idea how to throw a football in a spiral or balance on a skateboard like they did.

A ten-year-old's nightmare. Still, I was no worse off than the other children who were thought of as "misfits"—the girls who were too tall or too shy, the boy who was mildly hyperactive, the kids whose asthma excused them from PE.

There was one other child in my class, though, who reminded me of a different sort of pain. Her name was Coretta, and before my arrival she had been the only Black person in our grade. She was plump and dark-skinned and didn't seem to have many friends. From the first day, we avoided each other but watched from a distance, as if having contact would somehow make us feel even more different and alone.

Finally, during recess one hot, cloudless day, we found ourselves in the same corner of the playground. I don't remember what we said to each other, but I remember that suddenly she was chasing me around the jungle gyms and swings. She was laughing brightly, and I teased her and dodged this way and that, until she finally caught me and we fell to the ground breathless. When I looked up, I saw a group of children, faceless before the glare of the sun, pointing down at us.

"Coretta has a boyfriend! Coretta has a boyfriend!"

The chants grew louder as a few more kids circled us.

"She's not my g-girlfriend," I stammered. I looked to Coretta for help, but she just stood there looking down at the ground.

"Coretta's got a boyfriend! Why don't you kiss her, mister boyfriend?"

"I'm not her boyfriend!" I shouted. I ran up to Coretta and gave her a slight shove; she staggered back and looked up at me, but still said nothing. "Leave me alone!" I shouted again. And suddenly Coretta was running, faster and faster, until she disappeared from sight. Appreciative laughs rose around me. Then the bell rang, and the teachers appeared to round us back into class.

For the rest of the afternoon, I was haunted by the look on Coretta's face just before she had started to run: her disappointment that I had abandoned her. I wanted to explain to her somehow that it had been nothing personal; I'd just never had a girlfriend before and saw no particular need to have one now. But I didn't even know if that was true. I knew only that it was too late for explanations, that somehow I'd been tested and had failed. Whenever I snuck a glance at Coretta's desk, I saw her with her head bent over her work, pulled into herself and asking no favors.

After that, I was mostly left alone, like Coretta. I learned to speak less often in class so I wouldn't draw attention to myself. I made a few friends and managed to toss a wobbly football around. But from that day forward, a part of me felt crushed. After school let out, I would walk the five blocks to our apartment. If I had any change in my pockets, I might stop off at a newsstand run by a blind man, who would let me know what new comics had come in. Gramps would let me into the apartment, and as he lay down for his afternoon nap, I would watch cartoons and sitcom reruns. At four-thirty, I would wake Gramps and we would drive downtown to pick up Toot. My homework would be done in time for dinner, which we ate in front of the television. There I would stay for the rest of the evening, negotiating with Gramps over which shows to watch, sharing the latest snack food he'd discovered at the supermarket. At ten o'clock, I went to my room and fell asleep to the sounds of Top 40 music on the radio.

Snack food, TV, radio: Surrounded by all that, I somehow felt safe, as if I had dropped into a long hibernation. I wonder how long I might have stayed in that "sleep" had it not been for the telegram Toot found in the mailbox one day.

"Your father's coming to see you," she said. "Next month. Two weeks after your mother gets here. They'll both stay through New Year's."

She carefully folded the paper and slipped it into a drawer in the kitchen. Both she and Gramps fell silent. For a moment the air was sucked out of the room, and we stood alone with our thoughts.

"Well," Toot said finally, "I suppose we better start looking for a place where he can stay."

Gramps took off his glasses and rubbed his eyes.

"Should be one hell of a Christmas."

OVER LUNCH, I explained to a group of boys that my father was a prince.

"My grandfather, see, he's a chief. It's sort of like the king of the tribe, you know . . . like the Indians. So that makes my father a prince. He'll take over when my grandfather dies."

"What about after that?" one of my friends asked as we emptied our trays into the trash bin. "I mean, will you go back and be a prince?"

"Well . . . if I want to, I could. It's sort of complicated, see, 'cause the tribe is full of warriors. Like Obama . . . that means 'Burning Spear.' The men in our tribe all want to be chief, so my father has to settle these feuds before I can come."

As the words tumbled out of my mouth and I felt the boys warm up to me, a part of me really began to believe the story. But another part of me knew that I was telling a lie, something I'd constructed from the scraps of information I'd picked up from my mother.

In truth, I didn't know what to expect my father to be. He was still unknown, and vaguely threatening.

My mother sensed my nervousness in the days building up to his arrival—I think she felt the same. She tried to assure me that the reunion would go smoothly. They had written to each other while we were in Indonesia, and he knew all about me. Like her, my father had remarried, and I now had five brothers and one sister living in Kenya. He had been in a bad car accident, and this trip was part of his recuperation after a long stay in the hospital.

"You two will become great friends," she decided.

Along with news of my father, she began to stuff me with information about Kenya and its history. I'd stolen the name Burning Spear from a book she gave me about Jomo Kenyatta, the first president of Kenya. But in general I remembered little of what she told me. Only once did she really spark my interest, when she told me that my father's tribe, the Luo, were a "Nilotic" people who had moved to Kenya from their original home along the banks of the world's greatest river, the Nile. This seemed promising. Gramps still kept a painting he had once done: a replica of lean, bronze Egyptians on a golden chariot. I had visions of the great kingdoms of ancient Egypt I had read about, pyramids and pharaohs, queens with names like Nefertiti and Cleopatra.

One Saturday I went to the public library near our apartment and found a book on East Africa. There was only a short paragraph on the Luos. *Nilote,* it turned out, described a number of tribes that had originated in the Sudan along the White Nile, far south of the Egyptian empires. The Luo raised cattle and lived in mud huts and ate corn meal and yams and something called millet. Their traditional clothing was a leather thong across the crotch. There was no mention of pyramids. I left the book open on a table and walked out, crushed.

The big day finally arrived, and Miss Hefty let me out early from class, wishing me luck. My legs were heavy, and with each step toward my grandparents' apartment, the thump in my chest grew louder. When I entered the elevator, I stood without pressing the button. The door closed, then reopened, and an older Filipino man who lived on the fourth floor got on.

"Your grandfather says your father is coming to visit you today," the man said cheerfully. "You must be very happy."

Finally, when I could think of no possible way to escape, I rang the doorbell. Toot opened the door.

"There he is! Come on, Bar . . . come meet your father."

And there, in the unlit hallway, I saw him, a tall, dark figure who walked with a slight limp. He crouched down and put his arms around me, and I let my arms hang at my sides. Behind him stood my mother, her chin trembling as usual.

"Well, Barry," my father said. "It is a good thing to see you after so long. Very good."

He led me by the hand into the living room, and we all sat down.

"So, Barry, your grandmama has told me that you are doing very well in school."

I shrugged.

"He's feeling a little shy, I think," Toot offered. She smiled and rubbed my head.

"Well," my father said, "you have no reason to be shy about doing well. Have I told you that your brothers and sister have also excelled in their schooling? It's in the blood, I think," he said with a laugh.

I watched him carefully as the adults began to talk. He was much thinner than I had expected, the bones of his knees showing through his trousers. I couldn't imagine him lifting a man off the ground and holding him over a cliff. Beside him, a cane with an ivory head leaned against the wall. He wore a blue blazer, a white shirt, and a scarlet ascot. His horn-rimmed glasses reflected the light of the lamp, so I couldn't see his eyes very well, but when he took the glasses off to rub the bridge of his nose, I saw that they were slightly yellow, the eyes of someone who's had the disease malaria more than once. He looked fragile and tired.

After an hour or so, my mother suggested that he take a nap, and he agreed. He began to fish around in his travel bag until he finally pulled out three wooden figurines—a lion, an elephant, and an ebony man in a plumed headdress beating a drum—and handed them to me.

"Say thank you, Bar," my mother said.

"Thank you," I muttered.

My father and I both looked down at the carvings, lifeless in my hands. He touched my shoulder.

"They are only small things," he said softly. Then he nodded to Gramps, and together they gathered up his luggage and went downstairs to the apartment they'd rented for him.

A MONTH. THAT'S how long we had together. The five of us spent most evenings in my grandparents' living room. During the day we would drive around the island or take short walks past places my father wanted to show me: the lot where his apartment had once stood; the hospital where I had been born; my grandparents' first house in Hawaii. There was so much to tell in that single month, so much explaining to do, and yet when I reach back into my memory for the words of my father, they seem lost. I often felt mute when I was with him, and he never pushed me to speak. I'm left with mostly images that appear and fade: his head thrown back in laughter at one of Gramps's jokes; his grip on my shoulder as he introduces me to one of his old friends from college; the narrowing of his eyes, the stroking of his wispy goatee as he reads his important books.

I remember those images—and his effect on other people. Whenever my father spoke—one leg draped over the other, his large hands outstretched to direct or deflect attention, his voice deep and sure, sweet-talking and laughing—a sudden change took place in the family. Gramps became more vigorous and thoughtful, my mother more bashful; even Toot, who normally hid in her bedroom, would debate politics or finance with him, stabbing the air with her blue-veined hands to make a point. It was as if his presence brought back the hopeful spirit of earlier times. The last time my father was in Hawaii, Martin Luther King had not yet been shot; John F. Kennedy was president, his brother Robert still alive. Now, once again, it seemed that anything was possible so long as you had the courage to bring about change.

It fascinated me, this strange power of his, and for the first time I began to think of my father as something real and immediate, perhaps even permanent.

We did things together. At a concert by the jazz pianist Dave Brubeck, I struggled to understand the unusual chords and changes in tempo, watching my father carefully and clapping when he clapped. We stood in front of the Christmas tree and posed for pictures, the only ones I have of us together. I held an orange basketball he'd given to me, and he showed off the tie I'd bought him. ("Ah," he said when I gave it to him, "people will know that I am very important wearing such a tie.") Sometimes during the day I lay beside him in his sublet, reading my book while he read his. Although I did not feel I knew him any better, I began imitating his gestures and turns of phrase. I grew accustomed to his company.

After a couple of weeks, though, I could feel things getting more tense. Gramps complained that my father was sitting in his chair. Toot muttered, while doing the dishes, that she wasn't his servant. One evening, I turned on the television to watch a cartoon special—*How the Grinch Stole Christmas*—and all the whispers broke into shouts.

"Barry, you have watched enough television tonight," my father said. "Go in your room and study now, and let the adults talk."

Toot stood up and turned off the TV. "Why don't you turn the show on in the bedroom, Bar."

"No, Madelyn," my father said, "that's not what I mean. He has been watching that machine constantly, and now it is time for him to study."

My mother tried to explain that it was almost Christmas vacation, that the cartoon was a Christmas favorite, that I had been looking forward to it all week. "It won't last long."

"Anna, this is nonsense," my father said. "If the boy has done his work for tomorrow, he can begin on his next day's assignments. Or the assignments he will have when he returns from the holidays." He turned to me. "I tell you, Barry, you do not work as hard as you should. Go now, before I get angry at you."

I went to my room and slammed the door, listening as the voices outside grew louder, Gramps insisting that this was his house, Toot saying that my father had no right to come in and bully everyone, including me, after being gone all this time. I heard my father say that they were spoiling me, that I needed a firm hand, and I listened to my mother tell her parents that they were still interfering in her life. We all stood accused.

Even after my father left and Toot came in to say that I could watch the last five minutes of my show, I felt as if something had cracked open between all of us, goblins rushing out of some old, sealed-off lair. I watched the green Grinch who wanted to ruin Christmas but was touched to the heart by the faith of the little Whos of Whoville, and I thought: This is a lie. People don't change like that.

I began to count the days until my father would leave and things would return to normal.

The next day, Toot sent me down to the apartment where my father was staying to see if he had any laundry to wash. I knocked, and my father opened the door, shirtless. Inside, I saw my mother ironing some of his clothes. Her hair was tied back in a ponytail, and her eyes were soft and dark, as if she'd been crying. My father asked me to sit down beside him on the bed, but I told him that Toot needed me to help her, and left after giving him the message. Back upstairs, I had begun cleaning my room when my mother came in.

"You shouldn't be mad at your father, Bar. He loves you very much. He's just a little stubborn sometimes."

"Okay," I said without looking up. I could feel her eyes follow me around the room until she finally let out a slow breath and went to the door.

"I know all this stuff is confusing for you," she said. "For me, too. Just try to remember what I said, okay?" She put her hand on the doorknob. "Do you want me to close the door?"

I nodded, but she had been gone for only a minute when she stuck her head back into the room.

"By the way, I forgot to tell you that Miss Hefty has invited your father to come to school on Thursday. She wants him to speak to the class."

I couldn't imagine worse news. I spent that night and all

of the next day trying not to think about the inevitable: the faces of my classmates when they heard about mud huts, all my lies about chiefs and princes exposed, the painful jokes afterward. Each time I remembered, my body squirmed as if it had received a jolt to the nerves.

I was still trying to figure out how I'd explain myself when my father walked into our class the next day. Miss Hefty welcomed him eagerly, and as I took my seat I heard several children ask each other what was going on. I became more desperate when our math teacher, a big, no-nonsense Hawaiian named Mr. Eldredge, came into the room, followed by thirty confused children from his homeroom next door.

"We have a special treat for you today," Miss Hefty began. "Barry Obama's father is here, and he's come all the way from Kenya, in Africa, to tell us about his country."

The other kids looked at me as my father stood up, and I looked away, focusing on a tiny chalk mark on the blackboard behind him. He had been speaking for some time before I could finally bring myself back to the moment. He was leaning against Miss Hefty's thick oak desk and describing the deep gash in the earth where mankind had first appeared. He spoke of the wild animals that still roamed the plains, the tribes that still required a young boy to kill a lion to prove his manhood. He spoke of the customs of the Luo, how elders were respected more than anyone and made laws for all to follow. And he told us of Kenya's struggle to be free, how the British had wanted to stay and unjustly rule the people, just as they had in America; how many had been enslaved only because of the color of their skin, just as they had in America. But the Kenyans, like all of us in the room, longed to be free and develop themselves through hard work and sacrifice.

When he finished, Miss Hefty was beaming with pride. All my classmates applauded heartily, and a few struck up the courage to ask questions, each of which my father appeared to consider carefully before answering. The bell rang for lunch, and Mr. Eldredge came up to me.

"You've got a pretty impressive father."

The ruddy-faced boy who once asked me if in Africa they still ate people said, "Your dad is pretty cool."

And off to one side, I saw Coretta watch my father say good-bye to some of the children. She was concentrating too hard to smile; her face showed only a look of simple satisfaction.

TWO WEEKS LATER, my father was gone.

The day he left, as my mother and I helped him pack his bags, he dug up two records, in dull brown dust jackets.

"Barry! Look here—I forgot that I had brought these for you. The sounds of your continent."

It took him a while to figure out how my grandparents' old stereo worked, but finally the disk he chose began to turn, and he carefully placed the needle on the groove. There was a tinny guitar lick, then sharp horns, the thump of drums, then the guitar again, and then voices, clean and joyful. They seemed to be urging us on.

"Come, Barry," my father said. "You will learn from the master."

And suddenly his slender body was swaying back and forth, the lush sound was rising, his arms were swinging, and his feet were weaving over the floor. His bad leg was stiff but his rump was high, his head back, his hips moving in a tight circle. The rhythm quickened, the horns sounded, and his eyes closed in pleasure. Then one eye opened to peek down at me and his solemn face spread into a silly grin, and my mother smiled, and my grandparents walked in to see what all the commotion was about. I took my first tentative steps with my eyes closed: down, up, my arms swinging, the voices lifting me. As I follow my father into the sound, he lets out a quick shout, bright and high, a shout that leaves much behind and reaches out for more, a shout that cries for laughter.

I hear him still.

CHAPTER 4

Five years after my father's visit, I was in high school, and things had gotten complicated.

On the surface, things were going well enough. I was doing the things American kids do. I took a part-time job at a fast food restaurant. There were some mediocre report cards and a few calls to the principal. I dealt with acne, learned to drive, and thought a lot about girls. I made my share of friends at school and went on an occasional awkward date. Sometimes I puzzled over the change in my classmates' status. Some rose in popularity while others fell, depending only on how they looked or the make of their cars. I watched from the sidelines, relieved that my position steadily improved.

But all the while I was struggling inside. I was trying to raise myself to be a Black man in America, and no one around me seemed to know exactly what that meant.

I hung out a lot with a friend named Ray. He was two

years older than me, a senior who had moved from Los Angeles the year before when his father, who was in the army, was transferred. Despite the difference in age, we'd fallen into an easy friendship—it had a lot to do with the fact that together we made up almost half of Punahou's Black high school population.

I enjoyed his company. He had a warmth and brash humor that made up for his constant boasting about his life in L.A.—the women who supposedly still called him long-distance every night, his football triumphs, the celebrities he knew. I dismissed most of what he told me, but not all. It was true that he was one of the fastest sprinters in the Hawaiian islands. Some people even said he was good enough for the Olympics, in spite of the big stomach that quivered under his sweat-soaked jersey whenever he ran and left coaches shaking their heads in disbelief.

Ray was the one who told me about Black parties at the university or out on the army bases, and I counted on him to help me navigate my way around.

In return, I listened to him when he wanted to vent his frustrations. One day, we were having lunch and he declared that he wasn't going to any more school parties. He said he thought the girls at Punahou wouldn't look twice at Black men, that they were "A-1, USDA-certified racists."

"Maybe they're just looking at that big butt of yours," I said. "Man, I thought you were in training." I grabbed one his French fries.

"Get your hands out of my fries. Buy your own."

"Just 'cause a girl don't go out with you doesn't make her racist," I said.

"Don't be thick, all right? I'm not just talking about one time." He told me about asking out girls who turned him down and then hooked up with guys he thought had a lot less to offer.

"So, fine," he went on, ranting now. "I figure there're more fish in the sea. I go ask Pamela out. She tells me she ain't going to the dance. I say cool. Get to the dance, guess who's standing there, got her arms around Rick Cook. 'Hi, Ray,' she says, like she don't know what's going down. I mean, *Rick Cook!* That guy got nothing on me, right? Nothing."

He stuffed a handful of fries into his mouth. "It ain't just me, by the way. I don't see you doing any better."

Because I'm shy, I thought. But I would never admit that to Ray.

"Now, *Black* sisters would be all over us," he claimed.

"Well . . ."

"Well what? Listen, why don't you get more playing time on the basketball team, huh? At least two guys ahead of you ain't nothing, and you know it, and they know it. I seen you tear 'em up on the playground, no contest. Why wasn't I starting on the football squad this season, no matter how many passes the other guy dropped? Tell me we wouldn't be treated different if we were white. Or Japanese. Or Hawaiian. Or Eskimo!"

I understood what he was saying, but I didn't see it the same way.

"Yeah, it's harder to get dates because there aren't any Black girls around here," I admitted. "But that don't make the girls that are here all racist. Maybe they just want somebody that looks like their daddy, or their brother, or whatever, and we ain't it. I'm saying yeah, I might not get the breaks on the team that some guys get, but they play like white boys do, and that's the style the coach likes to play, and they're winning the way they play. I don't play that way.

"As for your greasy-mouthed self," I added, reaching for the last of his fries, "I'm saying the coaches may not like you 'cause you're a smart-mouthed Black man, but it might help if you stopped eating all them fries, making you look six months pregnant."

"Man, I don't know why you're making excuses for these folks," Ray said. "Your way of looking at it is *way* too complicated for me."

Maybe it was because I was raised among white people that I couldn't share Ray's easy answers. For three years I had lived with my mother and Maya in a small apartment a block away from Punahou. My mother had separated from Lolo and returned to Hawaii not long after I did to pursue a master's degree in anthropology, supporting the three of us with her student grant money. Sometimes, when I brought friends home after school, my mother would overhear them comment about the lack of food in the fridge or the less-than-perfect housekeeping, and she would pull me aside and let me know that she was a single mother going to school again and raising two kids, so baking cookies wasn't exactly one of her top priorities. She said she appreciated the fine education I was receiving at Punahou, but she wasn't going to put up with snotty attitudes from me or anyone else, was that understood?

It was understood.

Despite my desire for independence, the two of us remained close, and I did my best to help her out when I could, shopping for groceries, doing the laundry, looking after the knowing child that my sister had become.

But when my mother was ready to return to Indonesia to do research to earn her degree in anthropology, I told her there was no way I'd go back with her. I wasn't sure that Indonesia was the right place for me anymore, and I didn't want to be new all over again. I could live once more with my grandparents. They would leave me alone, I knew, so long as I kept my trouble out of sight. That was fine with me. Away from my mother, away from my grandparents, I could keep looking for the truth about what it meant to be Black in America.

My father's letters provided few clues. They arrived now and then, on a single blue page with gummed-down flaps that covered any writing at the margins. He would report that everyone was fine, praise my progress in school, and insist that my mother, Maya, and I were all welcome to come to Kenya and take our rightful place beside him whenever we wanted. From time to time he included advice, usually in the form of sayings I didn't quite understand ("Like water finding its level, you will arrive at a career that suits you"). I would respond promptly on a wide-ruled page, and his letters would end up in the closet, next to my mother's pictures of him.

Gramps had a number of Black male friends, mostly poker and bridge partners, and when I was younger I would let him drag me along to some of their games. They were old, neatly dressed men with hoarse voices and clothes that smelled of cigars. Whenever they saw me they'd give me a slap on the back and ask how my mother was doing, but once it was time to play they wouldn't say another word except to complain to their partner about a bid.

There was one who was different from the rest. He was a poet named Frank who lived in a dilapidated house in a run-down section of Waikiki. He'd lived in Chicago at the same time as the great Black writers Richard Wright and Langston Hughes, and he'd been somewhat well-known once himself. Gramps once showed me some of his work in an anthology of Black poetry. But by the time I met Frank he must have been nearly eighty, with a sagging face and an uncombed gray Afro that made him look like an old, shaggy-maned lion. He would read us his poetry whenever Gramps and I stopped by his house. But as the night wore on, the two of them would ask me to help them write dirty limericks. Eventually, they would complain about what a hard time they had getting along with women.

"If you let 'em, they'll drive you into your grave," Frank would tell me soberly.

I was intrigued by old Frank, who seemed to have some special, hard-earned knowledge, but the visits to his house always left me feeling uncomfortable. What was going on between him and Gramps, men who were so different in every way?

I had the same question whenever Gramps took me downtown to one of his favorite bars ("Don't tell your grandmother," he would say with a wink), where he would be the only white man in the place. Some of the men would wave at us, and the bartender, a big, light-skinned woman, would bring a Scotch for Gramps and a Coke for me. If nobody else was playing pool, Gramps would teach me the game. But usually I would sit at the bar, my legs dangling from the high stool, blowing bubbles into my drink and looking at the pictures of half-naked women on the wall. If he was around, a man named Rodney with a wide-brimmed hat would stop by to say hello.

"How's school coming, captain?"

"All right."

"You getting them *A*'s, ain't you?"

"Some."

"That's good. Sally, buy my man here another Coke," Rodney would say, peeling a twenty off a thick stack of bills.

I can still remember the excitement I felt during those evening trips: the dark room, the click of the cue ball, the jukebox flashing its red and green lights, the weary laughter of the men. Yet even then, as young as I was, I had already begun to sense that most of the people in the bar weren't there out of choice. They needed to drink to forget their troubles. What my grandfather was looking for were people who could help him forget his own troubles, people he believed would not judge him the way other white people might. Maybe the bar really did help him forget. But I knew he was wrong about not being judged. He didn't belong there. By the time I had reached junior high school I had learned to say no to Gramps's invitations. Whatever it was that I needed would have to come from some other source.

TV, movies, the radio: those were the places to start. Pop culture was color-coded, and from it a boy could learn a walk, a talk, a step, a style. I couldn't croon like Marvin Gaye, but I could learn to dance all the *Soul Train* steps. I couldn't pack a gun like the Black detective Shaft, but I could sure enough curse like the comedian Richard Pryor.

And I could play basketball, with a passion that surpassed my limited talent. My father's Christmas gift of a basketball had come at a time when the University of Hawaii team had slipped into the national rankings on the strength of an all-Black starting five the school had recruited from the mainland. That same spring, Gramps had taken me to one of their games, and I had watched the players in warm-ups. They were still boys, but to me at the time they looked like poised and confident warriors, chuckling to each other about some inside joke, glancing over the heads of fawning fans to wink at the girls on the sidelines, casually flipping layups or tossing high-arcing jumpers until the whistle blew and the centers jumped and the players joined in furious battle.

I decided to become part of that world, and began going down to a playground near my grandparents' apartment after school. From her bedroom window, ten stories up, Toot would watch me on the court until well after dark. I threw the ball with two hands at first, then developed an awkward jump shot and a crossover dribble. Hour after hour I'd be absorbed in the same solitary moves.

By the time I reached high school, I was playing on Punahou's teams, and could take my game to the university courts, where a handful of Black men would teach me an attitude that didn't just have to do with the sport. They let me know that respect came from what you did and not who your daddy was. That you could mouth off to rattle an opponent, but that you should shut up if you couldn't back it up. That you didn't let anyone sneak up behind you to see emotions—like hurt or fear—you didn't want them to see.

And they taught me something else, too, without even talking about it: a way of being together when the game was tight. Everyone, the best and worst players, would get swept up in the moment and go into a kind of group trance. In the middle of that you might make a move or a pass that surprised even you, so that even the guy guarding you had to smile in admiration.

When I look back on it now, deciding to play basketball seems like a pretty obvious choice for a Black kid—almost a cliché. But unlike the boys around me—the surfers, the football players, the would-be rock-and-roll guitarists—I didn't see that many options for myself. At that time, there just weren't a lot of ways for Black kids to connect with other people so that our race didn't remind us of our lack of status. But on the basketball court, being Black wasn't a disadvantage. We could put on a kind of costume and play a role and forget our uncertainty in every other part of life. It was on the court that I made my closest white friends. And it was there that I met Ray and the other Black kids close to my age who had begun to trickle into the islands, teenagers who were just as confused and angry as I was.

"That's just how white folks will do you," one of those Black friends might say when we were alone. Everybody would chuckle and shake their heads, and my mind would run down a list of slights. There was the boy in seventh grade who called me a coon; I could still see his tears of surprise—"Why'dya do that?"—when I gave him a bloody nose. There was the tennis pro who told me during a tournament that I shouldn't touch the schedule pinned up on the bulletin board because my color might rub off, and his thin-lipped, red-faced smile when I threatened to report him. ("Can't you take a joke?" he said.) There was the older woman in my grandparents' apartment building who became upset when I got on the elevator behind her and ran out to tell the manager that I was following her, and refused to apologize when she was told that I lived in the building. There was our assistant basketball coach, a young, wiry man from New York with a nice jumper, who, after a pick-up game with some talkative Black men, muttered within earshot of me and three of my teammates that we shouldn't have lost to a bunch of "niggers." When I told him—with a fury that surprised even me—to shut up, he calmly explained to me that "there are Black people, and there are niggers. Those guys were niggers."

It wasn't merely the cruelty that upset me; Black people could be mean, too. It was a particular brand of arrogance, a lack of awareness. It was as if white people didn't know they were being cruel in the first place. Or maybe they thought we deserved their scorn.

White folks. The term itself was uncomfortable in my mouth, like a foreign phrase. Sometimes I would be talking to Ray about *white folks* this or *white folks* that, and I would suddenly remember my mother's smile, and the words would seem awkward and false. Or I would be helping Gramps dry the dishes after dinner and Toot would come in to say she was going to sleep, and those same words— *white folks*—would flash in my head like a bright neon sign, and I would suddenly grow quiet, as if I had secrets to keep.

Later, when I was alone, I would try to untangle these difficult thoughts. It was obvious that certain white people could be exempted from the general category of our distrust:

Ray was always telling me how cool my grandparents were. The term *white* was simply a shorthand for him, I decided, a tag for what my mother would call a bigot. And although I recognized the risks in his terminology—how easy it was to fall into the same sloppy thinking my basketball coach had displayed when he said "there are Black people, and there are niggers"—Ray assured me that we would never talk about white people in front of white people without knowing exactly what we were doing, or there might be a price to pay.

But was that right? Was there still a price to pay for *us*? I would remind Ray that we weren't living in the South during segregation, where for so long, laws made sure that Black people and white people stayed separate. We weren't forced to live in some heatless housing project in Harlem or the Bronx. We were in Hawaii. We said what we pleased, ate where we pleased; we sat at the front of the bus. None of our white friends, guys like Jeff or Scott from the basketball team, treated us any differently than they treated each other. They loved us, and we loved them back. It seemed like half of them imitated Black NBA players like Doctor J, as if they wanted to be Black themselves.

Well, that's true, Ray would admit.

Maybe we could afford to give our angry pose a rest, I said. Save it for when we really needed it.

And Ray would shake his head. A pose, huh? Speak for your own self.

And I would know that Ray had flashed his trump card,

one that, to his credit, he rarely played. I was different, after all, potentially suspect; I had no idea who my own self was. Unwilling to risk exposure, I would quickly drop the subject.

Perhaps if we had been living in New York or L.A., I would have been quicker to pick up the rules of the high-stakes game we were playing. As it was, I learned to slip back and forth between my Black and white worlds, understanding that each possessed its own language and customs and structures of meaning, convinced that with a bit of translation on my part the two worlds would eventually cohere. Still, the feeling that something wasn't quite right stayed with me, a warning that sounded whenever a white girl mentioned in the middle of conversation how much she liked Stevie Wonder, or when a woman in the super-market asked me if I played basketball, or when the school principal told me I was cool. I did like Stevie Wonder, I did love basketball, and I tried my best to be cool at all times. So why did such comments always set me on edge? There was a trick there somewhere, although I couldn't quite figure out what the trick was, who was doing the tricking, and who was being tricked.

And I learned to slip back and forth between my Black and white worlds, convinced that even though each had its own language and customs, I could make them into one whole.

One day in early spring Ray and I met up after class and began walking in the direction of the stone bench that circled a big banyan tree on Punahou's campus. It was called the

Senior Bench, but it served mainly as a gathering place for the high school's popular crowd, the jocks and cheerleaders and partygoing set, with their jesters, attendants, and ladies-in-waiting jostling for position up and down the circular steps. One of the seniors, a stout defensive tackle named Kurt, was there, and he shouted loudly as soon as he saw us.

"Hey, Ray! Mah main man! Wha's happenin'!"

Ray went up and slapped Kurt's outstretched palm. But when Kurt repeated the gesture to me, I waved him off.

"What's his problem?" I overheard Kurt say to Ray as I walked away. A few minutes later, Ray caught up with me and asked me what was wrong.

"Man, those folks are just making fun of us," I said.

"What're you talking about?"

"All that 'Yo baby, give me five.'"

"So who's mister sensitive all of a sudden?" asked Ray. "Kurt don't mean nothing by it."

"If that's what you think, then hey—"

Ray's face suddenly lit up with anger, and we had a huge argument. For Ray, giving white people five and "talking your game" with them was how he got along—and who was I to interfere with that? He said it was different for me, that I had mastered the art of sucking up to the white teachers. ("Yes, Miss Snooty Teacher," he said, mocking me. "I just find this novel so engaging. And can I have just one more day for that paper?") Finally, he said, "It's their world, all right? They own it, and we in it." Then he stomped off.

By the following day, things had cooled down, and Ray suggested that I invite our friends Jeff and Scott to a party Ray was throwing at his house that weekend. I hesitated for a moment—we had never brought white friends along to a Black party—but Ray insisted, and I couldn't find a good reason to object. Neither could Jeff or Scott; they both agreed to come so long as I was willing to drive. And so that Saturday night, after one of our games, the three of us piled into Gramps's old Ford Granada and rattled our way out to Schofield Barracks, maybe thirty miles out of town.

When we arrived the party was well on its way, and we steered ourselves toward the refreshments. The presence of Jeff and Scott seemed to make no waves. Ray introduced them around the room, they made some small talk, and they took a couple of the girls out on the dance floor. But I could see right away that the scene had taken my white friends by surprise. They kept smiling a lot. They huddled together in a corner. They nodded self-consciously to the beat of the music and said "Excuse me" every few minutes. After maybe an hour, they asked me if I'd be willing to take them home.

"What's the matter?" Ray shouted over the music when I went to let him know we were leaving. "Things just starting to heat up."

"They're not into it, I guess."

Our eyes met, and for a long stretch we just stood there, the noise and laughter pulsing around us, Ray's gaze as unblinking as a snake's. Finally he put out his hand, and

I grabbed hold of it, our eyes still fixed on each other. "Later, then," he said, his hand slipping free from mine, and I watched him walk away through the crowd.

Outside the air had turned cool. The street was absolutely empty, quiet except for the fading tremor of Ray's stereo. In the car, Jeff put an arm on my shoulder, looking apologetic and relieved. "You know, man," he said, "that really taught me something. I mean, I can see how it must be tough for you and Ray sometimes, at school parties . . . being the only Black guys and all."

I snorted. "Yeah. Right."

Jeff meant well, but a part of me wanted to punch him right there. We rode in silence while I replayed in my mind the fight I'd had with Ray the day before. By the time I had dropped my friends off, I had begun to see a new map of the world, frightening in its simplicity. We were always playing on the white man's court, Ray had told me, by the white man's rules. If the principal, or the coach, or a teacher, or Kurt, wanted to spit in your face, he could, because he had power and you didn't. If he decided not to, if he treated you like a man or came to your defense, it was because he knew that the words you spoke, the clothes you wore, the books you read, your ambitions and desires, were still, in a way, dictated by him. Whatever he decided to do, it was his decision to make, not yours. The power had nothing to do with his motives or even his conscious feelings about Black people, so the distinction between "good whites" and "bad whites" didn't really mean all that much.

In this agitated frame of mind, I began to question everything that I thought was the free expression of my Black self. Had I *chosen* my own taste in music, my slang, my sense of humor, my basketball moves? Or was I hiding behind those things along with other Black people? This was scary logic. If you thought that way, then what were your options in life? You could withdraw into a smaller and smaller coil of rage, until "being Black" meant simply knowing that you were powerless and accepting defeat. It was a kind of prison you built for yourself. Or you could lash out at your "captors" and become what was called "a militant," someone who spoke out or acted in anger—which could get you thrown into a different kind of prison.

I NEEDED TO find out whether other Black people had shared this nightmare vision. So over the next few months I went to the library and gathered up books by James Baldwin, Ralph Ellison, Langston Hughes, Richard Wright, and W.E.B. Du Bois. At night I would close the door to my room, telling my grandparents I had homework to do, and there I would sit and read and struggle to figure out how someone with my peculiar beginnings fit into the world. But there was no escape to be had. In every page of every book, in Wright's Bigger Thomas and Ellison's Invisible Man, I kept finding the same anguish, the same doubt. No matter how learned or loving or ironic these writers were, there was still a kind of self-hatred. Their art couldn't help them in the end. All of them finally withdrew, exhausted and bitter—Du Bois to Africa, Baldwin to Europe, Hughes deep into Harlem.

Only Malcolm X's autobiography seemed to offer something different. Before he was murdered, he was always trying out new roles, creating himself over and over. His words had a blunt poetry. Above all, he insisted on respect and would work as hard as he could to get it. Yet he had another, angrier side, with talk of "blue-eyed devils" and apocalypse. I didn't pay much attention to that side of him; I knew he had abandoned that talk toward the end of his life. But one line in the book haunted me. He spoke of a wish to rid himself of whatever white blood ran through him. I knew he was serious. I also knew that his way could not be my way. My road to self-respect would never allow me to cut myself off from my mother and grandparents, my white roots.

Toward the end of his life, Malcolm seemed to hold out hope that some white people might live beside him in a distant future, in a far-off land. In the meantime, I looked to see where the people would come from who were willing to work toward this future and populate this new world.

ONE MORNING AROUND that time, I awoke to the sound of an argument in the kitchen—my grandmother's soft voice followed by my grandfather's deep growl. I opened my door to see Toot entering their bedroom to get dressed for work. I asked her what was wrong.

"Nothing. Your grandfather just doesn't want to drive me to work this morning, that's all."

When I entered the kitchen, Gramps was muttering under his breath. He poured himself a cup of coffee as I told him that I would be willing to give Toot a ride to work if he was tired. It was a bold offer, for I wasn't a morning person. He scowled at my suggestion.

"That's not the point. She just wants me to feel bad."

"I'm sure that's not it, Gramps."

"Of course it is." He sipped from his coffee. "She's been catching the bus ever since she started at the bank. She said it was more convenient. And now, just because she gets pestered a little, she wants to change everything."

Toot's tiny figure hovered in the hall, peering at us from behind her bifocals.

"That's not true, Stanley."

I took her into the other room and asked her what had happened.

"A man asked me for money yesterday. While I was waiting for the bus."

"That's all?"

Her lips pursed with irritation. "He was very aggressive, Barry. Very aggressive. I gave him a dollar and he kept asking. If the bus hadn't come, I think he might have hit me over the head."

I returned to the kitchen. Gramps was rinsing his cup, his back turned to me. "Listen," I said, "why don't you just let me give her a ride. She seems pretty upset."

"By a panhandler?"

"Yeah, I know—but it's probably a little scary for her, seeing some big man block her way. It's really no big deal."

He turned around and I saw now that he was shaking. "It *is* a big deal. It's a big deal to me. She's been bothered by men before. You know why she's so scared this time? I'll tell you why. Before you came in, she told me the fella was *Black*." He whispered the word. "That's the real reason why she's bothered. And I just don't think that's right."

The words were like a fist in my stomach.

Trying to calm myself down, I told him in my steadiest voice that such an attitude bothered me, too. But I said that Toot's fears would pass and that we should give her a ride in the meantime. Gramps slumped into a chair in the living room and said he was sorry he had told me. Before my eyes, he grew small and old and very sad. I put my hand on his shoulder and told him that it was all right, I understood.

We remained like that for several minutes, in painful silence. Finally he insisted that he drive Toot after all, and struggled up from his seat to get dressed. After they left, I sat on the edge of my bed and thought about my grandparents. They had sacrificed again and again for me. They had poured all their lingering hopes into my success. Never had they given me reason to doubt their love; I doubted they ever would. And yet I knew that men who might easily have been my brothers could still inspire their rawest fears.

THAT NIGHT, I drove into Waikiki, past the bright-lit hotels and down toward the Ala-Wai Canal. It took me a while to recognize the house, with its wobbly porch and low-pitched roof. Inside, the light was on, and I could see the old poet Frank sitting in his overstuffed chair, a book of verse in his lap, his reading glasses slipping down his nose. I sat in the car, watching him for a time, then finally got out and tapped on the door. The old man barely looked up as he rose to undo the latch. It had been three years since I'd seen him. He looked the same, his mustache a little whiter, his cut-off jeans with a few more holes and tied at the waist with a length of rope. He invited me inside.

"How's your grandpa?"

"He's all right."

"So what are you doing here?"

I wasn't sure. I told Frank some of what had happened.

"Funny cat, your grandfather," he said. "You know he and I grew up maybe fifty miles apart?"

I shook my head.

"We sure did. Both of us lived near Wichita. We didn't know each other, of course. I was long gone by the time he was old enough to remember anything. I might have seen some of his people, though. Might've passed 'em on the street. If I did, I would've had to step off the sidewalk to give 'em room. Your grandpa ever tell you about things like that?"

I shook my head again.

"Naw," Frank said, "I don't suppose he would have. Stan doesn't like to talk about that part of Kansas much. Makes him uncomfortable. He told me once about a Black girl they hired to look after your mother. A preacher's daughter, I think it was. Told me how she became a regular part of the family. That's how he remembers it, you understand—this girl coming in to look after somebody else's children, her mother coming to do somebody else's laundry. A regular part of the family."

Frank wasn't watching me; his eyes were closed now, his head leaning against the back of his chair, his big wrinkled face like a carving of stone. "You can't blame Stan for what he is," Frank said quietly. "He's basically a good man. But he doesn't *know* me. Any more than he knew that girl that looked after your mother. He *can't* know me, not the way I know him. Maybe some of these Hawaiians can, or the Indians on the reservation. They've seen their fathers humiliated, their mothers violated. But your grandfather will never know what that feels like. That's why he can come over here and drink my whiskey and fall asleep in that chair you're sitting in right now. Sleep like a baby. See, that's something I can never do in his house. *Never.* Doesn't matter how tired I get, I still have to watch myself, for my own survival."

Frank opened his eyes. "What I'm trying to tell you is,

your grandma's right to be scared. She's at least as right as Stanley is. She understands that Black people have a reason to hate. That's just how it is. For your sake, I wish it were otherwise. But it's not. So you might as well get used to it."

Frank closed his eyes again. His breathing slowed until he seemed to be asleep. I thought about waking him, then decided against it and walked back to the car. The earth shook under my feet, ready to crack open at any moment. I tried to steady myself.

I knew for the first time that I was utterly alone.

CHAPTER 5

By the time I got to eleventh grade, I had stopped writing to my father and he'd stopped writing back. My friend Ray had gone off to junior college somewhere and I had set the books aside. I had grown tired of trying to untangle a mess that wasn't of my own making.

I had learned not to care.

Marijuana helped, and booze. But when I drank or got high, it wasn't about proving what a down brother I was. I got high for just the opposite effect. It was something that could push questions of who I was out of my mind. I had discovered that it didn't make any difference whether you smoked weed in the white classmate's sparkling new van, in the dorm room of some brother you'd met down at the gym, or on the beach with a couple of Hawaiian kids who had dropped out of school. Nobody asked you whether your father was rich or poor. Everybody was welcome into the club of disaffection. And if the high didn't solve whatever it was that was getting you down, it could at least help you laugh and see through all the hypocrisy and cheap moralizing.

That's how it seemed to me then, anyway. It wasn't until my senior year that I saw the difference that color and money made after all, in who survived, how soft or hard the landing when you finally fell. Of course, either way, you needed some luck—just what my classmate Pablo didn't have. He'd been stopped by a cop and didn't have his driver's license, and the cop had nothing better to do than to check the trunk of his car. Then there was Bruce, who took too much LSD and wound up in a mental institution. And Duke, who didn't walk away from a car wreck.

I had tried to explain some of this to my mother once, the role of luck in the world, the spin of the wheel. It was at the start of my senior year in high school; she was back in Hawaii, her research in Indonesia completed, and one day she marched into my room, wanting to know the details of Pablo's arrest. I gave her a reassuring smile and patted her hand and told her not to worry, I wouldn't do anything stupid.

Except that she didn't seem reassured at all. She just sat there, studying my eyes, her face as grim as a hearse.

"Don't you think you're being a little casual about your future?" she said.

"What do you mean?"

"You know exactly what I mean. One of your friends was just arrested for drug possession. Your grades are slipping. You haven't even started on your college applications.

Whenever I try to talk to you about it you act like I'm just this great big bother."

I didn't need to hear all this. It wasn't like I was flunking out. I started to tell her how I'd been thinking about maybe not going away for college, how I could stay in Hawaii and take some classes and work part-time. She cut me off before I could finish.

"You could get into any school in the country," she said, "if you just put in a little effort. Remember what that's like? Effort? Come on, Bar, you can't just sit around like a good-time Charlie waiting for luck to see you through."

"A good-time what?"

"A good-time Charlie. A loafer."

I looked at her sitting there, so earnest, so certain of her son's destiny. I suddenly felt like puncturing that certainty of hers.

"A good-time Charlie, huh?" I laughed. "Well, why not? Maybe that's what I want out of life. I mean, look at Gramps. He didn't even go to college."

The comparison caught my mother by surprise. Her face went slack, her eyes wavered. It suddenly dawned on me that this was her greatest fear.

"Is that what you're worried about?" I asked. "That I'll end up like Gramps?"

She shook her head quickly. "You're already much better educated than your grandfather," she said. But the certainty had finally drained from her voice.

I FELT BAD after that conversation. I knew that on some level my mother was right. Drinking and taking drugs could never stop the ticking sound of the clock, the sound that life was passing by and all you had to show was emptiness. What I'd tried to explain to my mother was that her faith in justice and rational behavior was misplaced. I wanted to tell her that all the education and good intentions in the world couldn't give you the power to change the world's blind, mindless course.

Later we could look back on that conversation and laugh, because her worst fears hadn't come to pass. I had graduated right on time, had been accepted into several respectable schools, and had chosen Occidental College in Los Angeles, mainly because I'd met a California girl I liked while she was vacationing in Hawaii with her family.

But I was still just going through the motions. I didn't care that much about college, or anything else. Even Frank thought I had a bad attitude, although he was less than clear about how I should change it.

What had Frank called college? *An advanced degree in compromise.* I thought back to the last time I had seen the old poet, a few days before I'd left Hawaii. He had asked me what it was that I expected to get out of college. I told him I didn't know, and he shook his head.

"Well," he said, "that's the problem, isn't it? You *don't know.* You're just like the rest of these young cats out here.

All you know is that college is the next thing you're supposed to do. And the Black people who are old enough to know better, who fought all those years for your right to go to college—they're just so happy to see you in there that they won't tell you the truth. The real price of admission."

"And what's that?"

"Leaving your race at the door," he said. "Leaving your people behind." He studied me over the top of his reading glasses. "Understand something, boy. You're not going to college to get educated. You're going there to get *trained*. They'll train you to want what you don't need. They'll train you to manipulate words so they don't mean anything anymore. They'll train you to forget what it is that you already know. They'll train you so good, you'll start believing what they tell you about equal opportunity and the American way and all that shit. They'll give you a big office and invite you to fancy dinners, and tell you you're a credit to your race. Until you want to actually start running things, and then they'll yank on your chain and let you know that you may be a well-trained, well-paid nigger, but you're a nigger just the same."

"So what is it you're telling me—that I shouldn't be going to college?"

Frank's shoulders slumped, and he fell back in his chair with a sigh. "No. I didn't say that. You've got to go. I'm just telling you to keep your eyes open. Stay awake."

Keeping your eyes open wasn't as easy as it sounded. Not in sunny L.A., where I landed the following fall. Not as you strolled through Occidental's campus, a few miles from Pasadena, with its tree-lined streets and Spanish-tiled roofs. The students were friendly, the teachers encouraging. It was the fall of 1979, Jimmy Carter was on his way out, and Ronald Reagan was promising a new optimism, "morning in America." When you left campus, you drove on the freeway to Venice Beach or over to Westwood, passing the poor Black neighborhoods of East L.A. or South Central without even knowing it, just more palm trees peeking out like dandelions over the high concrete walls. L.A. wasn't all that different from Hawaii—not the part you saw, anyway. It was just bigger, and easier to find a barber who knew how to cut a Black man's hair.

Anyway, most of the other Black students at Oxy didn't seem all that worried about "compromise." There were enough of us on campus to constitute a tribe, and we stayed close together and traveled in packs. Freshman year, when I was still living in the dorms, we grumbled and complained about the same things Ray and I and other Black folks back in Hawaii had grumbled and complained about. Otherwise, our worries were the same as those of the white kids around us. Surviving classes. Landing a job that paid well after graduation. Meeting women. I had stumbled upon one of the well-kept secrets about Black people: that most of us weren't interested in revolt, that most of us were tired of thinking about race all the time. If we preferred to keep to ourselves, it was mainly because that was the easiest way to stop thinking about it. It was a lot easier than spending all your time mad or trying to guess what white folks were thinking about you.

So why couldn't *I* let the idea of race go?

I don't know. Maybe it was because I didn't come from a poor Black neighborhood like Compton or Watts. If you grew up there, just surviving was a revolutionary act. When you got to college, your family was back there rooting for you. They were happy to see you escape; there was no question of "betraying your race." I was more like the Black students who had grown up in the suburbs. You could spot them right away by the way they talked, the people they sat with in the cafeteria. They would tell you they weren't defined by the color of their skin. They were *individuals*.

That's how my friend Joyce liked to talk. She was good-looking, with green eyes, honey skin, and pouty lips. We lived in the same dorm my freshman year, and just about every Black guy at school was chasing her. One day I asked her if she was going to the Black Students' Association meeting. She looked at me funny, then started shaking her head like a baby who doesn't want what it sees on the spoon.

"I'm not Black," Joyce said. "I'm *multiracial*."

Then she started telling me about her father, who *happened* to be Italian and was the sweetest man in the world; and her mother, who *happened* to be part African and part French and part Native American and part something else. "Why should I have to choose between them?" she asked me. Her voice cracked, and I thought she was going to cry. "It's not white people who are making me choose. Maybe it used to be that way, but now they're willing to treat me like a person. No—it's *Black people* who always have to make everything racial. *They're* the ones making me choose. *They're* the ones who are telling me that I can't be who I am. . . ."

They, they, they. It seemed to me that people like Joyce often talked about the richness of their multicultural heritage and it sounded real good, until you noticed that they avoided Black people. It wasn't necessarily a conscious choice. White culture was everywhere, and they just gravitated toward it. They thought white people were the ones who didn't see everything in terms of race, who were willing to adopt someone a little more "exotic" into their ranks. Only white culture had individuals. If you chose Black culture, you'd be just another member of a "minority group," unwilling to think for yourself. So mixed-race people like Joyce or me would start to think, Why should we get lumped in with the losers if we don't have to be?

So you make your choice, pretending that you're not making a choice, and it works for a while—until an available taxi drives past you or the woman in the elevator clutches her purse, and you're outraged. Less fortunate Black people have to put up with such indignities every single day of their lives, but that's not why you're upset. You're upset because you're wearing an expensive suit and speak impeccable English. And yet you've somehow been mistaken for an ordinary nigger.

Don't you know who I am? I'm an *individual*!

THE FACT IS, I kept recognizing pieces of myself in Joyce and all the other Black kids who felt the way she did, and that's what scared me. I needed to put distance between them and me, to convince myself that I wasn't "compromised" the way Frank said I'd be—that I was indeed still awake.

To avoid being mistaken for a sellout, I chose my friends carefully. The more politically active Black students. The foreign students. The Chicanos. The Marxist professors and feminists and punk-rock performance poets. We smoked cigarettes and wore leather jackets. At night, in the dorms, we discussed the literature and philosophy of oppressed people, the history of European nations taking over small and less powerful countries. When we ground out our cigarettes in the hallway carpet or set our stereos so loud that the walls began to shake, we thought we were making a political statement against a "bourgeois" society that was stifling us.

Ironically, it was Black friends who made me rethink such dopey ideas. The first time I met Regina, for example, was when a brother named Marcus was giving me grief about my choice of reading material.

"Sister Regina," Marcus said. "You know Barack, don't you? I'm trying to tell Brother Barack here about this racist tract he's reading." Marcus held up a copy of Joseph Conrad's *Heart of Darkness*, which is about a white man in the late nineteenth century who travels deep into Central Africa and sets himself up as a kind of crazed king over the indigenous Black people living there.

"Man, stop waving that thing around," I said, and tried to snatch it out of his hands.

"Just being seen with a book like this makes you embarrassed, don't it?" he said. "I'm telling you, man, this stuff will poison your mind." He looked at his watch. "Damn, I'm late for class." He leaned over and pecked Regina on the cheek. "Talk to this brother, will you? I think he can still be saved."

Regina smiled and shook her head as we watched Marcus stride out the door. "Marcus is in one of his preaching moods, I see."

I tossed the book into my backpack. "Actually, he's right," I said. "It is a racist book. The way Conrad sees it, Africa's the cesspool of the world, Black folks are savages, and any contact with them breeds infection."

Regina blew on her coffee. "So why are you reading it?"

"Because it's assigned." I paused, not sure if I should go on. "And because the book teaches me things. About white people, I mean. See, the book's not really about Africa. Or Black people. It's about the man who wrote it. The European. The American. So I read the book to help me understand what it is about Black people that makes white people so afraid. It helps me understand how people learn to hate."

"And that's important to you," Regina said.

My life depends on it, I thought. But I didn't tell Regina that. I just smiled and said, "That's the only way to cure an illness, right? Diagnose it."

Regina smiled back and sipped her coffee. I had seen her around before, usually sitting in the library with a book in hand, a big, dark-skinned woman who wore stockings and dresses that looked homemade, along with tinted, oversized glasses and a scarf always covering her head. I knew she was a junior, helped organize Black student events, didn't go out much. She stirred her coffee idly and asked, "What did Marcus call you just now? Some African name, wasn't it?"

"Barack."

"I thought your name was Barry."

"Barack's my given name. My father's name. He was Kenyan."

"Does it mean something?"

"It means 'Blessed.' In Arabic. My grandfather was a Muslim."

Regina repeated the name to herself, testing out the sound. "Barack. It's beautiful." She leaned forward across the table. "So why does everybody call you Barry?"

"Habit, I guess. My father used it when he arrived in the States. I don't know whether that was his idea or somebody else's. He probably used Barry because it was easier to pronounce. You know—helped him fit in. Then it got passed on to me. So I could fit in."

"Do you mind if I call you Barack?" Regina asked.

I smiled. "Not as long as you say it right."

We ended up spending the afternoon together, talking and drinking coffee. Regina told me about her childhood in Chicago. Her father had left, her mother struggled to pay the bills. Their apartment building on the South Side was never warm enough in winter and got so hot in the summer that people went out by the lake to sleep. She told me about the neighbors on her block, about walking past bars and pool halls on the way to church on Sunday. She told me about evenings in the kitchen with uncles and cousins and grandparents, their voices bubbling up in laughter. Her own voice evoked a vision of Black life in all its possibility, a vision that filled me with longing—a longing for place, for a life I had never known. As we were getting up to leave, I told Regina I envied her.

"For what?" she asked.

"I don't know. For your memories, I guess."

Regina laughed, a round, full sound from deep in her belly.

"What's so funny?"

"Oh, Barack," she said, catching her breath, "isn't life something? And here I was all this time wishing I'd grown up in Hawaii."

STRANGE HOW A single conversation can change you. I felt my true, honest voice returning to me that afternoon with Regina. As time went by, I could feel it growing stronger, sturdier, a bridge between my future and my past. I began to remember my values, simple things I'd heard from my mother and grandparents, from TV sitcoms and philosophy books. Things like: Look at yourself before you pass judgment. Don't make someone else clean up your mess. Don't get so wrapped up in your perceived injuries, because it's not always about *you*.

Now I was hearing the same things from Black people I respected, people who had more excuses for being bitter than I'd ever had. My new friends made me realize that my ideas about who I was and who I might become had grown stunted and narrow and small—that the values that mattered weren't Black or white.

My identity might begin with the fact of my race, but it didn't, couldn't, end there.

At least, that's what I would choose to believe.

IN MY SOPHOMORE year at Occidental, I got involved in the national campaign to pressure colleges to stop investing money in South Africa, where Black people were kept down by the cruel system known as apartheid. At first, I was just following the lead of my politically active friends. But as the months passed, I noticed that people began to listen to my opinions, and I became hungry for words—words that could carry a message, support an idea. There was a meeting of the school's trustees coming up, the people who decided where the college would invest its money, and our group decided to plan a rally outside the administration building. When somebody suggested me as the first speaker at the rally, I quickly agreed. I figured I was ready, and could reach people where it counted.

It was going to be a kind of street theater, a little play to dramatize how hard it was for activists in South Africa to protest injustice. I was only supposed to make a few opening remarks and then a couple of white students would come onstage dressed in paramilitary uniforms and drag me away.

I had helped plan the script, but when I sat down to prepare what I would say, something happened. In my mind it became more than a two-minute set-up, more than a way to prove I was down with the politics of protest. I started to remember my father's visit to Miss Hefty's class, the look on Coretta's face that day, and the power of my father's words to *transform* people. With the right words, I thought, everything could change—South Africa, the lives of ghetto kids just a few miles away, my own shaky place in the world.

I was still in that trancelike state when I mounted the stage, the sun in my eyes, in front of a few hundred restless students who had just come from lunch. A couple of them were throwing a Frisbee on the lawn; others were standing off to the side, ready to head off to the library at any moment. I stepped up to the microphone.

"There's a struggle going on," I said. My voice barely

carried beyond the first few rows. A few people looked up, and I waited for the crowd to quiet.

"I say, there's a struggle going on!"

The Frisbee players stopped.

"It's happening an ocean away. But it's a struggle that touches each and every one of us. Whether we know it or not. Whether we want it or not. A struggle that demands we choose sides. Not between Black and white. Not between rich and poor. No—it's a harder choice than that. It's a choice between dignity and servitude. Between fairness and injustice. Between commitment and indifference. A choice between right and wrong . . ."

I stopped. The crowd was quiet now, watching me. Somebody started to clap. "Go on with it, Barack," somebody else shouted. "Tell it like it is." Then the others started in, clapping, cheering, and I knew I had them, that the connection had been made.

Then I felt someone's hands grabbing me from behind. It was just as we'd planned it, my white friends in uniforms looking grim behind their dark glasses. They started yanking me off the stage, and I was supposed to act like I was trying to break free, except a part of me wasn't acting. I really wanted to stay up there.

I had so much left to say.

CHAPTER 6

I spent my first night in Manhattan curled up in an alleyway.

It wasn't intentional. While still in L.A., I'd arranged to rent an apartment in Spanish Harlem, near Columbia University, from a friend of a friend who was moving out. After dragging my luggage through the airport, the subways, Times Square, and across 109th from Broadway to Amsterdam, I finally stood at the door, a few minutes past ten p.m.

I pressed the buzzer repeatedly, but no one answered. The street was empty, the buildings on either side boarded up. Eventually, a young Puerto Rican woman emerged from the building, throwing a nervous look my way before heading down the street. I rushed to catch the door before it slammed shut, and, pulling my luggage behind me, proceeded upstairs to knock, and then bang, on the apartment door. Again, no answer, just a sound down the hall of some scared resident's deadbolt lock being thrown into place.

New York. Just like I pictured it. I checked my wallet—not enough money for a motel. I knew one person in New York, a guy named Sadik I'd met in L.A., but he'd told me that he worked all night at a bar somewhere. With nothing to do but wait, I carried my luggage back downstairs and sat on the stoop. After a while, I reached into my back pocket and pulled out the letter from my father that I was carrying. It had been sent from Kenya.

Dear Son,

It was such a pleasant surprise to hear from you after so long. I am fine and doing all those things which you know are expected of me in this country. I just came back from London where I was attending to Government business, negotiating finances, etc. In fact it is because of too much travel that I rarely write to you. In any case, I think I shall do better from now on.

You will be pleased to know that all your brothers and sisters here are fine, and send their greetings. Like me, they approve of your decision to come home after graduation. When you come, we shall, together, decide on how long you may wish to stay. Barry, even if it is only for a few days, the important thing is that you know your people, and also that you know where you belong.

Please look after yourself, and say hallo to
your mum, Tutu, and Stanley. I hope to hear from
you soon.

Love, Dad

I folded the letter up and stuffed it back into my pocket. It hadn't been easy to write him; our correspondence had all but died over the past four years. In fact, I had gone through several drafts when composing my reply, crossing out lines, struggling to find the right tone, resisting the impulse to explain too much. "Dear Father." "Dear Dad." "Dear Dr. Obama." And now he had answered me, cheerful and calm. Know where you belong, he advised. He made it sound simple, like calling directory assistance.

"Information—what city, please?"

"Uh . . . I'm not sure. I was hoping you could tell me. The name's Obama. Where do I belong?"

Maybe it really was that simple for him. I imagined my father sitting at his desk in Nairobi, Kenya's largest city, a big man in government, with clerks and secretaries bringing him papers to sign, a minister calling him for advice, a loving wife and children waiting at home, his own father's village only a day's drive away. The image made me vaguely angry, and I tried to set it aside, concentrating instead on the sound of salsa coming from an open window somewhere down the block. The same thoughts kept returning to me, though, as persistent as the beat of my heart. Where did I belong?

Two years from graduating college, I had no idea what I was going to do with my life, or even where I would live. Hawaii lay behind me like a childhood dream; I could no longer imagine settling there. Whatever my father might say, I knew it was too late to ever truly claim Kenya as my home. And even though I had come to understand myself as a Black American, I had no community, no place where I could put down stakes and test my commitment to my people.

And so, when I heard about a transfer program that Occidental had arranged with Columbia, I'd been quick to apply. I figured that even if there weren't any more Black students at Columbia than there were at Oxy, there would at least be Black neighborhoods close by. Maybe New York would turn out to be the place where I belonged. There wasn't much in L.A. to hold me back. Most of my friends were graduating that year. Regina was on her way to Spain for a study-abroad program, and Marcus had dropped out, disappeared.

Now here I was, with no place to stay the night. It was well past midnight by the time I crawled through a nearby fence that led to an alleyway. I found a dry spot, propped my luggage beneath me, and fell asleep.

IN THE MORNING, I woke up to find a white hen pecking at the garbage near my feet. Across the street, a homeless man was washing himself at an open hydrant and didn't object when

I joined him. There was still no one home at the apartment, but Sadik answered his phone when I called him and told me to catch a cab to his place on the Upper East Side.

He was a short, well-built Pakistani who had come to New York from London two years earlier and now made a living waiting on tables—yet another member of New York's huge undocumented-immigrant workforce.

"So tell me, what brings you to our fair city, Barry?" he asked when we sat down together.

I told him it was "Barack" now, and tried to explain the summer I'd just had, that I'd been brooding over the state of the world and the state of my soul. "I want to make amends," I said. "Make myself of some use."

"Well, amigo . . . you can talk all you want about saving the world, but this city tends to eat away at such noble sentiments. Look out there." He gestured to the crowd along First Avenue. "Everybody is looking out for number one. Survival of the fittest. Tooth and claw. That, my friend, is New York. But . . . who knows? Maybe you'll be the exception. In which case I will doff my hat to you."

In the coming months he watched me as I traveled, like a large lab rat, through the byways of Manhattan. He tried not to grin when I gave up a seat in the subway to a middle-aged woman but a burly young man jumped into it instead. He took me to fancy department stores and watched my eyes pop at the price tags on winter coats. He put me up when I eventually left the apartment on 109th because there wasn't any heat. And he accompanied me to Housing Court when the people who sublet me my next apartment ran off with my deposit.

"Tooth and claw, Barack. Stop worrying about the rest of these bums and figure out how you're going to make some money out of this fancy degree you'll be getting."

When Sadik lost his own lease, we moved in together. After a few months, he began to realize that the city had indeed had an effect on me. But not the one he'd expected. I gave up smoking pot. I ran three miles a day after my classes and fasted on Sundays. For the first time in years, I applied myself to my studies and kept a journal of daily reflections and very bad poetry. Whenever Sadik tried to talk me into going to a bar, I'd make some lame excuse.

"You're becoming a bore," he said.

He was right. In a way, I was proving what he'd said about the city's power to corrupt people. It was 1981. Wall Street was booming and men and women barely out of their twenties were getting ridiculously rich. There seemed no limits on what people desired—a more expensive restaurant, a finer suit of clothes, a more exclusive nightspot, a more beautiful woman, a more potent high. The beauty, the filth, the noise, the excess, all of it dazzled my senses. I wasn't certain I could resist those temptations, so I went to the other extreme.

But there was something else that made me keep this world at arm's length. I could sense that it was becoming more fractured. I had seen worse poverty in Indonesia and as much violence in L.A.; I had grown accustomed, everywhere, to suspicion between the races. But whether because of New York's density or because of its scale, here, you could see more clearly the rifts between races and classes, and the ferocity of the wars between the various tribes. In the stalls of Columbia's bathrooms, no matter how many times the administration tried to paint them over, the walls remained etched with graffiti like "nigger" and "kike."

It was as if all middle ground had collapsed. And nowhere was that collapse more apparent than in the Black community I had so lovingly dreamed of belonging to. One day I met a Black friend at his Midtown law firm and looked out from his high-rise office window, imagining a good life for myself—work I enjoyed, a family, a home. Until I noticed that he was the only Black lawyer in the firm. All the other Black people in the office were messengers or clerks.

I visited Harlem. I played on basketball courts I'd read about, I sat in the back pews of Abyssinian Baptist Church and was lifted by the gospel choir's sweet, sorrowful song. I caught a fleeting glimpse of the world I sought. But I couldn't find a place there to live. The elegant brownstones of Sugar Hill were occupied—and too expensive anyway. The few decent rental buildings in the neighborhood had ten-year waiting lists. What remained were rows and rows of uninhabitable tenements, in front of which young men selling drugs counted out their rolls of large bills, and winos slouched and stumbled and wept softly.

At first, I took all this as a personal affront, as if someone were mocking my ambitions to bring my worlds together. But people who had lived in New York for a while told me there was nothing original about my experience. The city was out of control, they said. But so long as I earned a bit of money, I'd be free to live like most middle-class Black residents of Manhattan. Never mind Harlem. I could choose a more polished style of clothing, better restaurants, and a more upwardly mobile group of friends.

I sensed, though, that those choices could end up being permanent. I'd probably send my kids to private school and take cabs at night to avoid the dangerous subways. I'd probably decide I needed a building with a doorman. And pretty soon I'd be on the other side of the line, unable to cross back over.

Unwilling to make that choice, I spent a year walking from one end of Manhattan to the other. I studied the range of human possibility. I looked at other people's lives and wondered if I could see in them a reflection of my own future.

IT WAS IN this humorless mood that my mother and sister found me when they came to visit during my first summer in New York.

"He's so skinny," Maya said to my mother.

"He only has two towels!" my mother shouted as she inspected the bathroom. "And three plates!" They both began to giggle.

They stayed with Sadik and me for a few nights, then moved to a condominium on Park Avenue that a friend of my mother's had offered them while she was away.

I had found a summer job clearing a construction site on the Upper West Side, so my mother and sister spent most of their days exploring the city on their own. When we met for dinner, they would give me detailed reports of their adventures: eating strawberries and cream at the Plaza Hotel, taking the ferry to the Statue of Liberty, visiting the Cézanne exhibition at the Metropolitan Museum of Art. I would eat in silence until they were finished and then launch into a long speech about the problems of the city and the politics of the people who had nothing. When the two of them withdrew to the kitchen, I would overhear Maya complaining to my mother.

"Barry's okay, isn't he? I hope he doesn't lose his cool and become one of those freaks you see on the streets."

One evening, my mother saw a newspaper ad for a movie called *Black Orpheus* and insisted we go see it that night.

"That was the first foreign film I ever saw!" she said. "I was only sixteen. I'd just been accepted to the University of Chicago—Gramps hadn't told me yet that he wouldn't let me go—and I was there for the summer, working as an au pair. It was the first time that I'd ever been really on my own. Gosh, I felt like such an adult. And when I saw this film, I thought it was the most beautiful thing I had ever seen."

Black Orpheus was a Brazilian film made in the 1950s, a breakthrough in its day. The cast was almost totally Black, yet it had won an international following. The story was simple: It was the Greek myth of ill-fated lovers Orpheus and Eurydice, only it was set in the favelas of Rio during the boisterous annual Carnival. In Technicolor splendor, the black- and brown-skinned Brazilians sang and danced and strummed guitars like carefree birds in colorful plumage.

About halfway through the movie, I decided that I'd seen enough. The movie depicted Black people as childlike—almost the reverse image of Joseph Conrad's dark savages—and I turned to my mother to see if she might be ready to go. But her face, lit by the blue glow of the screen, was wistful, melancholy. At that moment, I felt as if I were being given a window into her youthful heart. I realized that those images of childlike Black people were what my mother had carried with her to Hawaii all those years before. They were the simple but forbidden fantasies of a white, middle-class Kansas girl. Here was the promise of another life: warm, sensual, exotic, *different.*

I turned away, embarrassed for her, wondering whether emotions between people of different races could ever be pure. Even love was tarnished by the desire to find in the other person some element that was missing in ourselves.

For the next several days, I tried to avoid situations where my mother and I might be forced to talk. Then, a few days before she and Maya were about to leave, I stopped by their apartment. She noticed a letter addressed to my father in my hand.

"You guys arranging a visit?"

I told her that I had begun making plans to go to Kenya.

"Well, I think it'll be wonderful for you two to finally get to know each other," she said. "He was probably a bit tough for a ten-year-old to take, but now that you're older . . ."

I shrugged. "Who knows?"

She stuck her head out of the kitchen. "I hope you don't resent him."

"Why would I?"

"I don't know."

We sat there for a while, listening to the sounds of traffic below. Then, without any prompting, my mother began to retell an old story, in a distant voice, as if she were telling it to herself.

"It wasn't your father's fault that he left, you know. I divorced him. When we got married, your grandparents weren't happy. But they said okay—they probably couldn't have stopped us anyway, and they eventually came around to the idea that it was the right thing to do.

"Then Barack's father—your grandfather Hussein— wrote Gramps this long, nasty letter saying that he didn't approve of the marriage. He didn't want the Obama blood sullied by a white woman, he said. Well, you can imagine how Gramps reacted to that. And then there was a problem with your father's first wife . . . he had told me they were separated, but it was a village wedding, so there was no legal document that could show a divorce. . . ."

Her chin began to tremble, and she bit down on her lip, steadying herself. She said, "Your father wrote back, saying he was going ahead with it. Then you were born, and we agreed that the three of us would return to Kenya after he finished his studies. But your grandfather Hussein was still writing to your father, threatening to have his student visa revoked. By this time Toot had become hysterical—she had read about the rebellion in Kenya a few years earlier, which Western newspapers really played up—and she was sure I'd have my head chopped off and you'd be taken away.

"Even then, it might have worked out. Your father received two scholarship offers. One was to the New School, here in New York. The other was to Harvard. The New School agreed to pay for everything—room and board, a job on campus, enough to support all three of us. Harvard just agreed to pay tuition. But Barack was so stubborn, he just had to go to Harvard. 'How can I refuse the best education?' he asked. That's all he could think about, proving that he was the best."

She sighed, running her hands through her hair. "We were so young, you know. I was younger than you are now. He was only a few years older than that. Later, when he came to visit us in Hawaii, he wanted us to come live with him. But I was still married to Lolo, and his third wife had just left him, and I just didn't think . . ."

She stopped and laughed. "Did I ever tell you he was late for our first date? He asked me to meet him in front of the university library. When I got there he hadn't arrived, but

I figured I'd give him a few minutes. It was a nice day, so I lay down on one of the benches, and before I knew it I had fallen asleep. Well, an hour later—an hour!—he shows up with a couple of his friends. I woke up and the three of them were standing over me, and I heard your father saying, serious as can be, 'You see, gentlemen. I told you that she was a fine girl, and that she would wait for me.'"

My mother laughed once more, and once again I saw her as the child she had been. Except this time I saw something else: In her smiling, slightly puzzled face, I saw what all children *must* see at some point if they are going to grow up: their parents' lives revealed to them as separate and apart from their own. I saw their lives before their marriage and my birth. I saw their lives unfurling back to grandparents and great-grandparents, an infinite number of chance meetings, misunderstandings, projected hopes, limited circumstances.

My mother was the girl with *Black Orpheus,* the movie full of beautiful Black people, in her head, flattered by my father's attention, confused and alone, trying to tear herself away from her parents' grip. The innocence she carried that day, waiting for my father, was rooted in misconceptions and her own needs. But perhaps that's how any love begins, with impulses and cloudy images of someone else that help us break out of our solitude. And if we're lucky, those clouds will be transformed into something solid, something that will last.

In the movie theater, I'd decided that emotions between the races would never be pure, but my mother's words shook me out of that certainty. What I heard from my mother that day, speaking about my father, was something most Americans don't believe can exist between Black and white: the love of someone who knows your life in the round, through and through, a love that will survive disappointment. It was a love so generous that she tried to help me—the child who never knew him—see him with her eyes.

A FEW MONTHS later, the call came.

"Barry? Barry, is this you?"

The line was thick with static.

"Yes . . . Who's this?"

"Yes, Barry . . . this is your Aunt Jane. In Nairobi. Can you hear me?"

"I'm sorry—who did you say you were?"

"Aunt Jane. Listen, Barry, your father is dead. He is killed in a car accident. Hello? Can you hear me? I say, your father is dead. Barry, please call your uncle in Boston and tell him. I can't talk now, okay, Barry. I will try to call you again. . . ."

That was all.

When I phoned and told my mother that my father had died, I heard her cry out over the distance. Yet I felt no pain, and saw no reason to pretend otherwise. I didn't go to the funeral. I wrote to my father's family in Nairobi to express my condolences and asked them to write back. I wondered how they were doing. But my plans to travel to Kenya were placed on indefinite hold.

ANOTHER YEAR WOULD pass before I would meet my father, in my dreams.

I was traveling by bus with friends whose names I've forgotten. We rolled across deep fields of grass and hills that bucked against an orange sky.

An old white man, heavyset, sat beside me with a book that said the way we treat the elderly in our society is a test of our very souls. He told me he was on a trip to meet his daughter. I dozed and woke up to find everyone gone.

I got off the bus and found myself inside a building made of rough stone. A lawyer spoke to a judge. The judge said my father had spent enough time in jail, that it was time to release him. But the lawyer objected vigorously. He said laws are laws and we must maintain order.

Then I was standing before his cell. I opened the padlock and set it carefully on a window ledge. My father was before me, with only a cloth wrapped around his waist. He was very thin, with his large head and slender frame, his hairless arms and chest. He looked pale, his black eyes luminous against his ashen face.

"Look at you," he said. "So tall—and so thin. Gray hairs, even!" And I saw that it was true, and I walked up to him and we embraced. I began to weep, and felt ashamed, but could not stop myself.

"Barack. I always wanted to tell you how much I love you," he said. He seemed small in my arms now, the size of a boy.

He sat at the corner of his cot and set his head on his clasped hands and stared away from me, into the wall. Sadness spread across his face. I tried to joke with him; I told him that if I was thin it was only because I took after him. But when I whispered that we could leave together, he shook his head and told me it would be best if I left.

I awoke still weeping, my first real tears for him—and for me, his jailor, his judge, his son. I turned on the light and dug out his old letters. I remembered his only visit—the basketball he had given me and how he had taught me to dance. And I realized how even in his absence his strong image had given me something to live up to.

I stepped to the window and looked outside, listening to the first sounds of morning—the growl of the garbage trucks, footsteps in the apartment next door.

I knew I needed to search for him, to talk with him again.

PART TWO

CHICAGO

CHAPTER 7

I n 1983, I decided to become a community organizer.

There wasn't much detail to the idea; I didn't know anyone making a living that way. When my classmates in college asked just what a community organizer *did*, I couldn't answer them directly. Instead, I'd talk about the need for change: change in a White House that was indifferent to too many people's needs, in a Congress too obedient and corrupt, in a country too moody and self-absorbed to see what was going on. Change won't come from the top, I would say. Change will come from getting people to act at a grassroots level inside their own communities.

And my friends, Black and white and brown, would congratulate me for my high ideals and then go off and apply to graduate school in the hope of one day making real money.

I couldn't really blame them.

Looking back, I can see a certain logic in wanting to be a

community organizer. I still carried memories of Indonesia with its beggars and farmers, and of my stepfather, Lolo, who tried but was finally powerless to change the system.

But at the time, I was operating mainly on impulse, like a salmon swimming blindly upstream. In classes, I might dress up that impulse with slogans and theories I'd found in books. But at night, when I lay in bed, those theories would drift away and be replaced by romantic images of a past I had never known.

They were images of the civil rights movement, mostly, the grainy black-and-white footage that appears every February during Black History Month, the ones my mother showed me as a child. A pair of college students, hair short, backs straight, placing their orders at a lunch counter or standing on a porch in Mississippi, trying to convince a family of sharecroppers to register to vote. A county jail bursting with children, their hands clasped together, singing freedom songs.

Such images bolstered my spirits in a way that words never could. They told me that I wasn't alone in my struggles.

They also told me that I shouldn't take the existence of the Black community for granted. Communities had to be created, fought for, tended like gardens. They got bigger or smaller based on our dreams. And the dreams of the people who marched and went to jail for civil rights had been large.

You weren't automatically a member of a community. You had to earn your membership through shared sacrifice.

Perhaps, if I worked hard enough, I could speak for the promise of a larger, more inclusive American community, Black, white, and brown—one in which the uniqueness of my own life would be accepted.

That was my idea of organizing. It was a promise of redemption.

And so, in the months leading up to my graduation from Columbia, I wrote to every civil rights organization I could think of, to any Black elected official in the country with a progressive agenda, to neighborhood councils and tenant rights groups.

When no one wrote back, I wasn't discouraged. I decided to find more conventional work for a year, to pay off my student loans and maybe even save a little bit. Organizers didn't make any money.

Eventually a branch of a large corporation hired me as a research assistant. As far as I could tell I was the only Black man in the company, a source of shame for me but one of considerable pride for the secretaries. They treated me like a son, those Black ladies; they told me how they expected me to run the company one day. Sometimes, over lunch, I would tell them about all my wonderful organizing plans, and they would smile and say, "That's good, Barack," but the look in their eyes told me they were secretly disappointed.

Only Ike, the gruff Black security guard in the lobby, was willing to come right out and tell me I'd be making a mistake.

"Organizing? That's some kinda politics, ain't it? Why you wanna do something like that?"

I tried to explain the importance of mobilizing the poor and giving back to the community. But Ike just shook his head. "Mr. Barack," he said, "I hope you don't mind if I give you a little bit of advice. Forget about this organizing business. We don't need more folks running around here, all rhymes and jive. You can't help folks that ain't gonna make it nohow, and they won't appreciate you trying. Folks that wanna make it, they gonna find a way to do it on they own.

"Do something that's gonna make you some money. Not greedy, you understand. But enough. That's what we need, see. I'm telling you this 'cause I can see potential in you. Young man like you, got a nice voice—hell, you could be one of them announcers on TV. Or sales . . . got a nephew about your age making some real money there. How old are you?"

"Twenty-two."

"See there. Don't waste your youth, Mr. Barack. Wake up one morning, an old man like me, and all you gonna be is tired, with nothing to show for it."

I DIDN'T PAY Ike much attention at the time; I thought he sounded too much like my grandparents. But as the months passed I felt the idea of becoming an organizer slipping away from me. The company promoted me. I had my own office, my own secretary, money in the bank. Sometimes I would catch my reflection in the elevator doors—see myself in a suit and tie, a briefcase in my hand—and for a split second I would imagine myself as a big-shot executive, barking out orders, closing deals, before I remembered who it was that I had told myself I wanted to be. At those moments I felt guilty.

Then one day, as I sat down at my computer to write an article on interest rates, something unexpected happened. My half sister Auma called.

We had written to each other occasionally but had never met. I knew that she had left Kenya to study in Germany, and in our letters we had mentioned the possibility of my going there for a visit, or perhaps her coming to the States. But the plans had always been left vague—neither of us had any money, we would say; maybe next year.

Now, suddenly, I heard her voice for the first time. It was soft and deep, tinged with a British accent from years of Kenya's colonial rule. She was coming to the States, she said, on a trip with several friends. Could she come to see me in New York?

"Of course," I said. "You can stay with me; I can't wait." And she laughed, and I laughed, and then the line grew quiet with static and the sound of our breath.

"Well," she said, "I can't stay on the phone too long, it's so expensive." And we hung up quickly after that, as if our contact were a treat to be doled out in small measures.

Two days before she was scheduled to arrive, Auma called again, her voice barely a whisper.

"I can't come after all," she said. "One of our brothers, David . . . he's been killed. In a motorcycle accident. I don't know any more than that." She began to cry. "Oh, Barack. Why do these things happen to us?"

I tried to comfort her as best I could. I asked her if I could do anything for her. I told her there would be other times for us to see each other. Eventually her voice quieted; she had to go book a flight home to Kenya, she said.

"Okay, then, Barack. See you. Bye."

After she hung up, I left my office, telling my secretary I'd be gone for the day. For hours I wandered the streets of Manhattan, the sound of Auma's voice playing over and over in my mind. A continent away, a woman cries. On a dark, dusty road, a boy skids out of control, tumbling against hard earth, wheels spinning to silence. Who were these people, I asked myself, these strangers who carried my blood?

I STILL WONDER how that first contact with Auma and the news of David's death changed my life. I don't know. But Auma's voice reminded me that I had wounds that I could not heal myself. A few months later, I resigned from the company and threw myself back into the search for an organizing job.

An offer came from a well-known civil rights outfit with a board of directors that had ten white executives and one Black minister. They wanted someone Black and educated and self-assured enough to feel comfortable in corporate boardrooms—just where I didn't want to be. I declined their offer.

I passed out flyers for an assemblyman's race in Brooklyn. The candidate lost and I never got paid.

I had all but given up when I received a call from a guy named Marty Kaufman. He explained that he'd started an organizing project in Chicago and was looking to hire a trainee. When he met me in New York, his appearance didn't inspire much confidence. He was a white man of medium height wearing a rumpled suit over a pudgy frame. His face was heavy with a two-day-old beard; behind a pair of thick, wire-rimmed glasses, his eyes were set in a perpetual squint. He asked why someone from Hawaii wanted to be an organizer. "You must be angry about something," he said, and added that this was actually a good thing. Anger, he said, was a requirement for the job. "Well-adjusted people find more relaxing work."

Marty was trying to pull urban Black people and suburban white people together around a plan to save manufacturing jobs in metropolitan Chicago. He needed somebody to work with him, he said. Somebody Black.

"Most of our work is with churches," he said. "With the unions in such bad shape, they're the only game in town. Churches are where the people are, and that's where the values are. Pastors won't work with you, though, just out of the goodness of their hearts. They'll give a sermon on

Sunday. But they won't really move unless you can show them how it'll help them pay their heating bill."

Marty asked me what I knew about Chicago.

I thought for a moment. "Hog butcher to the world," I said finally, dredging up a line from poet Carl Sandburg's 1914 ode to the city, which was known for its slaughterhouses.

Marty shook his head. "The butcheries closed a while ago."

"The Cubs never win," I offered.

"True."

"America's most segregated city," I said. "A Black man, Harold Washington, was just elected mayor, and white people don't like it."

"So you've been following Harold's career," Marty said. "I'm surprised you haven't gone to work for him."

"I tried," I admitted. "His office didn't write back."

Marty smiled and took off his glasses, cleaning them with the end of his tie. "Well, that's the thing to do, isn't it, if you're young and Black and interested in social issues? Find a political campaign to work for. A powerful patron— somebody who can help you with your own career. And Harold's powerful, no doubt about it. Lots of charisma. He has the support of the entire Black community, plus about half the Hispanics and a handful of white liberals. But you're right about one thing. The atmosphere in the city is polarized—people have taken sides and won't budge. A big media circus. Not much is getting done."

"And whose fault is that?"

Marty put his glasses back on and met my stare. "It's not a question of fault," he said. "It's a question of whether any politician, even somebody with Harold's talent, can do much to break the cycle."

Marty offered to start me off at ten thousand dollars the first year, with a two-thousand-dollar travel allowance to buy a car; the salary would go up if things worked out.

On the way home, I stopped to sit on a nearby park bench and think about my options. A young Black boy shouted, "Excuse me, mister. You know why sometimes the river runs that way and sometimes it goes this way?"

I said it probably had to do with the tides, and that seemed to satisfy him.

As I watched him disappear, I realized I had never noticed which way the river ran.

A week later, I loaded up my car and drove to Chicago.

CHAPTER 8

arrived in July, and the sun sparkled through the deep green trees. The boats were out of their moorings, their distant sails like the wings of doves across Lake Michigan. Marty had told me that he would be busy those first few days, and so I was left on my own. I bought a map and took a tour of the city.

As I drove, I remembered the history I'd learned: the whistle of the Illinois Central Railroad, bearing the weight of the thousands of formerly enslaved people and their descendants who had come up from the South for better opportunities during the Great Migration; and the Black men and women and children, dirty from the soot of the railcars, clutching their battered luggage, making their way to the Promised Land. I passed a mail carrier and imagined he was the great novelist Richard Wright, delivering mail before his first book sold. I imagined Gramps's friend Frank in a baggy suit in front of the old Regal Theater, waiting to see jazz great Duke Ellington. The little girl with the glasses and pigtails could have been Regina, skipping rope.

One day I happened to pass Smitty's Barbershop, a fifteen-by-thirty-foot storefront on the edge of Hyde Park. The door was propped open when I walked in, the barbershop smells of hair cream and antiseptic mingling with the sound of men's laughter and the hum of slow fans. Smitty turned out to be an older Black man, gray-haired, slender and stooped. His chair was open and so I took a seat, soon joining in the familiar barbershop banter of sports and women and yesterday's headlines.

There was a picture of Chicago's new mayor, Harold Washington, on the wall, and the men talked about him with as much affection as if he were a relative. Smitty noticed me looking at the photo and asked if I'd been in Chicago during the election.

"Had to be here before Harold to understand what he means to this city," Smitty said. "Before Harold, seemed like we'd always be second-class citizens."

"Plantation politics," a man with a newspaper said.

"That's just what it was, too," Smitty said. "A plantation. Black people in the worst jobs. The worst housing. Police brutality out of control."

Clumps of hair fell into my lap as I listened to the men recall Harold's rise. He had run for mayor once before but hadn't gotten anywhere. The lack of support in the Black community was a source of shame, the men told me. But

Harold had tried again, and this time the people were ready. They had turned out in record numbers on election night, ministers and gang members, young and old.

And their faith had been rewarded. Smitty said, "The night Harold won, people just ran the streets. People weren't just proud of Harold. They were proud of themselves. I stayed inside, but my wife and I, we couldn't get to bed until three, we were so excited. When I woke up the next morning, it seemed like the most beautiful day of my life. . . ."

Smitty's voice had fallen to a whisper, and everyone in the room began to smile.

From a distance, reading the newspapers back in New York, I had shared in their pride. But something was different about what I was hearing now; there was an intensity in Smitty's voice that seemed to go beyond politics.

"Had to be here to understand," he had said. He'd meant here in Chicago; but he could also have meant here in his shoes, an older Black man who still burns from a lifetime of insults, of foiled or abandoned ambitions.

I asked myself if I could truly understand that. I believed that I could. The men thought I could, too. But would they feel the same way if they knew more about me? I tried to imagine what would happen if Gramps walked into the barbershop at that moment, how the talk would stop at the sight of a white man, how the spell would be broken, how they'd begin seeing me differently.

Smitty handed me the mirror to check his handiwork,

then pulled off my smock and brushed off the back of my shirt. "Thanks for the history lesson," I said, standing up.

"Hey, that part's free. Haircut's ten dollars. What's your name, anyway?"

"Barack."

He took the money and shook my hand. "Well, Barack, you should come back a little sooner next time. Your hair was looking awful raggedy when you walked in."

LATE THAT AFTERNOON, Marty picked me up in front of my new apartment and we headed to the southeast side of Chicago, past rows of small houses made of gray clapboard or brick, until we arrived at a massive old factory that stretched out over several blocks.

"The old Wisconsin Steel plant," Marty announced.

We sat there in silence, studying the building. It was empty and rust-stained, an abandoned wreck. On the other side of the chain-link fence, a spotted, mangy cat ran through the weeds.

"All kinds of people used to work in the plant," Marty said. "Black. White. Hispanic. All working the same jobs. All living the same kind of lives. But outside the plant, most of them didn't want anything to do with each other."

"So what makes you think they can work together now?"

"They don't have any choice," Marty said. "Not if they want their jobs back."

As we reentered the highway, Marty began to tell me

more about the organization he'd built. With the help of a sympathetic Catholic bishop, he'd met with area pastors and church members, and heard both Black and white congregants talk about their shame of unemployment, their fear of losing a house or being cheated out of a pension— their shared sense of having been betrayed.

Eventually more than twenty churches had agreed to form a coalition. I would specifically be working with representatives from parishes inside Chicago, an arm of Marty's organization that was called the Developing Communities Project, or DCP. And while things hadn't moved quite as fast as Marty had hoped, the group had just won their first real victory: the Illinois legislature had agreed to spend $500,000 helping out-of-work people find jobs. That was where we were going now, Marty explained. To a rally to celebrate the program.

"It's going to take a while to rebuild manufacturing out here," he said. "At least ten years. We'll have a stronger position when we get the unions involved. In the meantime, we just need to give people some short-term victories. Something to show them how much power they have once they stop fighting each other and start fighting the real enemy."

I asked who that was.

"The investment bankers. The politicians. The fat cat lobbyists."

It was twilight by the time we crossed the city line and pulled into the parking lot of a large suburban school, where crowds of people were already making their way into the auditorium: laid-off steelworkers, secretaries, and truck drivers, men and women who smoked a lot and didn't watch their weight, shopped at Sears or Kmart, drove late-model cars from Detroit and ate at Red Lobster on special occasions.

Marty hurried into the auditorium, but when I tried to follow, my way was blocked by three Black women. One of them, a pretty woman with orange-tinted hair, leaned over to me and whispered, "You're Barack, aren't you?"

"Don't he look clean-cut, Mona?" she said to one of her companions.

"Sure does!"

"Don't get me wrong," said the first woman. "I've got nothing against Marty. But the fact is, there's only so far you can—"

At that point, Marty waved at us from the stage. "You guys can talk to Barack all you want later. Right now I need all of you up here with me."

The woman with the orange hair was Angela. The other two were Mona and Shirley. We would end up spending a lot of time together.

The auditorium was almost filled, two thousand people in all, about a third of them Black residents bused in from the city. A choir sang two gospel songs, and there was a procession of speakers, ending with the governor, who offered his solemn pledge of support for the new job bank.

To my mind the whole thing came off a bit flat and staged, like a bad TV wrestling match. Still, the crowd seemed to be enjoying itself. And seeing all these Black and white faces together in one place, I felt cheered. I was sure I recognized in myself the same vision driving Marty. He believed that if you could just clear away the politicians and media and bureaucrats and give everybody a seat at the table, then ordinary people could find common ground. These were the first stirrings of something I would need in the months and years ahead: faith.

THE DAY AFTER the rally, Marty decided it was time for me to do some real work, and he handed me a long list of people to interview.

"Find out their self-interest," he said. "That's why people get involved in organizing—because they think they'll get something out of it."

At first I was worried that people might not be willing to talk with me, but once we met in person I found they didn't mind a chance to air their opinions about a do-nothing alderman or a neighbor who refused to mow his lawn. I heard certain things again and again. Most of the people in the area had been raised in cramped Black neighborhoods. They had few options. For most of its history, Chicago had been a city with many "restrictive covenants": private legal agreements among white homeowners not to sell or rent their properties to Black people. The people I talked to had some fond memories of the neighborhoods they'd built, which were like self-contained worlds, but they also remembered how there had never been enough heat or light or space to breathe—that, and the sight of their parents grinding out life in physical labor.

A few had followed their parents into the steel mills or onto the assembly line. But more had found jobs as mail carriers, bus drivers, teachers, and social workers—in the public sector, where laws against racial discrimination were more strongly enforced. Such jobs had benefits and provided enough security for them to think about buying homes. And with the passage of fair housing laws, which helped keep landlords and homeowners from refusing to rent or sell to Black people, they moved, one at a time, into white neighborhoods. Not because they were necessarily interested in mingling with white people, they told me, but because the houses were affordable, with small yards for their children; the schools were better and the stores cheaper. Maybe they also bought them just because they *could*.

Often, as I listened to these stories, I was reminded of the ones that Gramps and Toot and my mother had told—stories of hardship and migration, the drive for something better. But there was an inescapable difference. In these new stories, white families fled when Black families arrived, For Sale signs cropping up like dandelions under a summer sun. Stones flew through the windows of Black families' homes, and anxious parents could be heard calling their children indoors from innocent games. Entire blocks turned over in less than six months; entire neighborhoods in less than five years.

In these stories, wherever Black and white met, the result was sure to be anger and grief.

The area had never fully recovered from this racial upheaval. The stores and banks had left along with their white customers, and city services had declined. Still, when the Black families who'd now lived in their homes for ten or fifteen years looked back on the way things had turned out, they did so with some satisfaction. On the strength of two incomes, they had paid off house and car loans, maybe paid for college educations for their sons or daughters. They had kept their homes up and kept their children off the streets; they had formed block clubs to make sure that others did too.

It was when they spoke of the future that their voices sounded worried. The better their children did, the more likely they were to move away. In their place came younger, less stable families who couldn't always afford to keep up with their mortgage payments. Car thefts were up; churches had fewer members; the leafy parks were empty. Now there were loud groups of teenage parents feeding potato chips to crying toddlers, the discarded wrappers blowing down the block. People put bars on their doors to keep out burglars; they wondered if they could afford to sell their houses for less than they'd paid and retire to a warmer climate, perhaps move back to the South.

The parents with younger kids had even more difficult decisions. Ruby Styles was one of them. Her son, Kyle, was a bright but shy boy who was starting to have trouble at school. One of his friends had been shot right in front of his house. The boy was all right, but Ruby was worried about her own son's safety. Gang activity was on the rise.

Ruby introduced me to other parents who shared her fears and felt frustrated that the police were slow to respond. When I suggested that we invite the district police commander to a neighborhood meeting so they could share their concerns with him, everyone thought it was a good idea. Some pastors agreed to help us get the word around.

The meeting was a disaster. Only thirteen people showed up, scattered across rows of empty chairs. The district commander canceled on us and sent a "community relations" officer instead. Every few minutes an older couple would walk in looking for the Bingo game. I spent most of the evening directing them upstairs, while Ruby sat glumly onstage, listening to the police officer lecture about the need for parental discipline.

After that, I worried that Ruby might back away from organizing, but instead she threw herself headlong into our project, working hard to build a network of neighbors and school parents. She was what every organizer dreams of—someone with untapped talent, smart, steady, excited by the idea of a public life, eager to learn.

It was, surprisingly, some of the Baptist churches that resisted my efforts most. At a meeting with local pastors, I was introduced to a man named Reverend Smalls. He was tall and pecan-colored, with straightened hair that was swept back in a pompadour. He said, "Listen, Obama, the last thing we need is to join up with a bunch of white money and Catholic churches and Jewish organizers to solve our problems. White folks come in here thinking they know what's best for us, hiring a bunch of high-talking college-educated brothers like yourself who don't know any better. All they want to do is take over."

He told me that with Harold Washington in office, things would change. Black people had a direct line to City Hall now, and they could organize their own protests. Then he patted me on the shoulder and said he knew I meant well. "You're just on the wrong side of the battle right now," he said.

Marty laughed when I described my interaction with Reverend Smalls. "I told you the city's polarized," he said. "You should be glad you learned your lesson early."

Which lesson was that? I wondered. The one that says that America's historic civil-rights gathering in the 1960s in front of the Lincoln Memorial is only a distant memory— that in the end, we each pray to our own masters?

Marty and Reverend Smalls did share one thing. They knew that the more certain you were that your point of view was right, the more forceful you could be and the more power you could win. The problem was that one person's certainty always threatened another's, so none of those certain people could work with one another.

Meanwhile, all I had was doubt—and a job I wasn't sure I was up to doing.

CHAPTER 9

The place that symbolized everything I was fighting to
change was the Altgeld Gardens public housing project.

It sat at Chicago's southernmost edge: two thousand
apartments arranged in a series of two-story brick buildings
with army-green doors and grimy mock shutters. Everybody
called it the Gardens for short, but most of the children
who lived there grew up without ever having seen an actual
garden. It sat between the largest landfill in the Midwest and
a sewage treatment plant that gave off a heavy, putrid odor
that seeped through windows no matter how tightly they
were shut. Now that jobs from once-thriving factories were
gone, it seemed only natural to use the land as a dump.

A dump—and a place to house poor Black folks.

Good people, reformers, had once dreamed of building
decent housing for the poor. But politicians fought to
keep those places as far away as possible from white
neighborhoods. People who had jobs didn't want to live

there. Those who did were often miserable. Gradually, things began to fall apart.

Altgeld wasn't as bad as some of Chicago's high-rise projects, with their ink-black stairwells and urine-stained lobbies and random shootings. If you went inside the apartments at Altgeld, you would often find them well-kept, with small touches—a patterned cloth thrown over torn upholstery, a calendar with tropical beach scenes on the wall—that expressed the lingering idea of home.

But the place seemed in a perpetual state of disrepair. Ceilings crumbled, pipes burst, toilets backed up. The Chicago Housing Authority was supposed to maintain it, but city officials had stopped even pretending that repairs would happen anytime soon.

Pulling up at a church for one of my first meetings as an organizer at Altgeld, I closed my eyes and leaned my head against the car seat, feeling like the first mate on a sinking ship.

I was there to meet some of the neighborhood's key leaders—including Angela, Shirley, and Mona—and talk about getting things back on track. They were spirited, good-humored women, those three. Without husbands to help, they'd somehow managed to raise sons and daughters, juggle an assortment of part-time jobs, and organize Girl Scout troops, fashion shows, and summer camps for the parade of children that wandered through their church every day.

But that fall day morale was low, and they were angry,

especially about the new job bank that we had announced with such excitement the night of the rally. The government had picked a state university out in the suburbs to run the program, but its computers constantly malfunctioned. People were sent to interview for jobs that didn't exist. Two months after it was supposed to have started, no one had found work. Marty was furious, and at least once a week he would drive out to the university and try to pry answers from university officials. But the women from Altgeld weren't interested in Marty's frustrations. They complained that he wouldn't listen to their suggestions. All they knew was that $500,000 meant to fund the job bank's operation had gone to the white suburbs—and that their neighborhood had gotten nothing.

Marty said they were sore because he'd refused to hire them to run the program. "If you're going to do this work, Barack, you've got to stop worrying about whether people like you. They won't."

That day, I found the women waiting for me with long faces.

"We're quitting," Angela announced. "We're just tired. We've been at this for two years and we've got nothing to show for it."

I started to say that we just needed more time, but Shirley cut me off. "We don't have more time," she said. "We can't keep on making promises to our people and then have nothing happen."

Outside, a group of young boys were tossing stones at the boarded-up window of a vacant apartment, their hoods pulled over their heads. Part of me felt like joining them, tearing apart the whole dying landscape, piece by piece. Instead, I asked Angela, "What will happen to those boys out there? Who's going to make sure they get a fair shot? The politicians? The social workers? The gangs?"

I told them I'd come to Chicago because Marty had said there were people serious about changing their neighborhoods and the least they could do was give me a chance. "If you don't think anything's happened after working with me, I'll be the first to tell you to quit," I went on, my voice rising. "But if you're all planning to quit now, then answer my question: *What will happen to those boys?*"

There was a long silence. The boys moved on down the street. Shirley got more coffee.

Angela said, "I guess we could give it a few more months."

WINTER CAME AND the city turned monochrome—black trees against gray sky above white earth. Night now fell in mid-afternoon, especially when the snowstorms rolled in.

The work was tougher in such weather. Mounds of fine white powder blew through the cracks of my car, down my collar, and into the openings in my coat. As I journeyed around the city interviewing people, I never spent enough time in one place to thaw out, and the snow made it hard to find parking. When we held evening meetings, people often didn't show up; they called at the last minute to say they had the flu or their car wouldn't start. Those who did come looked damp and resentful.

Marty suggested that I take more time off, build a life for myself away from the job. His concerns were professional, he explained: Without support outside the work, an organizer could lose perspective and could quickly burn out. There was something to what he said. On weekends, I usually ended up alone in an empty apartment, making do with the company of books.

But gradually, the bonds between myself and the leaders working in our organization grew stronger, and I found them offering more than simple friendship. After meetings, I might go with one of the men to a local bar to watch the news or listen to oldies thump from a dinged-up corner jukebox. On Sunday, I'd go to church and let the women tease me over my confusion with communion and prayer. At a Christmas party, I danced with Angela, Mona, and Shirley and swapped sports stories with husbands who had been reluctantly dragged to the affair. I counseled sons or daughters on their college applications and played with grandchildren who sat on my knee.

At times like that I began to understand the true meaning of the work I had chosen. I remember sitting with a woman named Mrs. Stevens, waiting for a meeting to start.

I didn't know her well—only that she was very interested in renovating the local hospital.

Trying to make small talk, I asked her why she was so concerned with improving health care in the area; her family seemed healthy enough. Then she told me how, in her twenties, she was working as a secretary but had cataracts so bad that her doctor declared her legally blind. She had kept this from her boss for fear of being fired. Day after day, she snuck off to the bathroom to read her boss's memos with a magnifying glass, memorizing each line before she went back to type them up, staying at the office long after others had left. She kept this up for a year, until she finally saved enough money for an operation.

That's what these leaders were teaching me, day by day: a strength of spirit I hadn't imagined. They told me stories that were like explanations of their core selves. Stories full of terror and wonder, events that still haunted or inspired them. Sacred stories.

And it was this realization, I think, that finally allowed me to share more of myself with the people I was working with, to break out of the isolation that I had carried with me to Chicago. At first I was afraid that my experiences in Hawaii or Indonesia would sound too strange, that South Siders would be disturbed by how different I was. Instead, they would nod and laugh and offer a story to match mine—a lost father, a teenage brush with crime, a moment of simple grace.

Not to say that all these stories cheered my heart.

Sometimes I came face to face with a different, destructive kind of force.

One day just before Christmas, Ruby stopped by my office. From the minute she walked in, I thought I saw something different about her, but I couldn't quite put my finger on what it was. Finally, I realized that her eyes, normally a warm, dark brown that matched the color of her skin, had turned an opaque shade of blue, as if someone had glued plastic buttons over her irises.

"What did you do to your eyes?"

"Oh, these." Ruby shook her head and laughed. "They're just contacts, Barack. You like them?"

"Your eyes looked just fine the way they were."

"It's just for fun," she said, looking down, suddenly embarrassed. "Something different, you know."

For the rest of the day and into the next, I thought about Ruby's blue eyes. I had handled the moment badly and made her feel ashamed. After all, she wasn't someone who spent much time or money on herself—she was entitled to a bit of vanity. I realized that a part of me expected her and the other leaders to be immune to the images that bombard us all and make us insecure—the slender models in the fashion magazines, the square-jawed men in fast cars, the blondes with radiant blue eyes. I was vulnerable to those images, too, but somehow I had believed that Ruby and the others would be able to rise above such doubts about their own appearance.

When I mentioned the incident to a Black woman friend,

she stated the issue more bluntly. "What are you surprised about?" she said impatiently. "That Black people still hate themselves?"

No, I told her, I wasn't surprised. Since my discovery of bleaching creams in that magazine I had read in the American embassy in Jakarta, I'd become familiar with color consciousness in the Black community—good hair, bad hair; thick lips or thin; if you're light, you're all right, if you're Black, get back.

At the same time, I'd learned not to put too much stock in those who said "self-esteem" was the cure for all our ills, whether they were talking about substance abuse or teen pregnancy or Black-on-Black crime. "Self-esteem" was a vague, easy phrase for the hurts we'd been keeping to ourselves. But what exactly did it *mean*? Did you dislike yourself because of your color or because you couldn't read and couldn't get a job? Was the sense of emptiness you felt because of your kinky hair or the fact that your apartment had no heat or decent furniture? Everything was muddled together.

Perhaps with more self-esteem fewer Black people would be poor, I thought. But wouldn't it be better to concentrate on things besides skin tone and eye color, things we might all agree on, things we could control? Give that Black man some skills and a job. Teach that Black child reading and arithmetic in a safe, well-funded school. With the basics taken care of, each of us could search for our own sense of self-worth.

That's what I'd been thinking—until Ruby and her contact lenses shook me up. Maybe I was so focused on improving the practical realities of Black people's lives that I had not given enough weight to the hurt and distortions that lingered inside us all. Every day I saw and heard evidence of that kind of self-hatred. A Black leader casually explained that he never dealt with Black contractors: "A Black man'll just mess it up, and I'll end up paying white folks to do it all over again." Another said she couldn't mobilize people in her church because "Black folks are just lazy—don't wanna do nothing."

Often the word *nigger* replaced *Black* in such remarks. It was a word I'd always thought Black people used ironically, to prove we were so resilient that we could make fun of the way others put us down. That was until the first time I heard a young mother use it on her child to tell him he wouldn't amount to anything. That was until I heard teenage boys use it to wound one another. Even when Black people used it, the word's original meaning never completely went away. One of our defenses against being hurt is to strike out at ourselves first.

Those sacred stories I had been hearing of courage and sacrifice and overcoming great odds had a dark side: Most of them were the result of people's struggle against hate. And buried deep within those people, even the ones who had triumphed, was an image of the white people who had kept them down. Sometimes there was a single white face.

But sometimes there was just the faceless image of a system claiming power over our lives.

Could the bonds of our community be restored without rejecting the ghostly figure that haunted Black dreams? Could Ruby ever love herself without hating blue eyes?

RAFIQ AL-SHABAZZ HAD settled such questions in his mind and had built his career in Chicago on encouraging distrust of white people. He was a slight, wiry man with a goatee and a skullcap, a former gang member who had formed an organization he said was dedicated to Black empowerment and economic development. According to Rafiq, his coalition, based in Roseland, a largely Black, economically struggling neighborhood, had been critical to helping Mayor Washington get elected. From what my community leaders told me, however, Rafiq spent most of his time intimidating local businesses and elected officials into giving him small contracts to supply "community outreach" and other vaguely defined ventures. In fact, it was only after we had already negotiated with the City of Chicago to open a new job training center that Rafiq called me up and launched into a rapid-fire monologue.

"We gotta talk, Barack," he said. "What y'all are trying to do with job training needs to fit into the overall comprehensive development plan I've been working on. Can't think about this thing in isolation . . . got to look at the big picture. You don't understand the forces at work out here. Is big, man. All kinds of folks ready to stab you in the back."

Despite my doubts, I didn't want to shut people like Rafiq out, and we formed an uneasy alliance. It didn't go over too well with my colleagues. During group discussions, he would interrupt to rant about conspiracies and about Black people selling their own out, and everyone else would fall silent, not quite knowing what to say.

When the two of us were alone, though, Rafiq and I could sometimes have normal conversations, and I came to admire his determination and boldness. He confirmed that he had been a gang leader growing up in Altgeld Gardens. Then he had found religion, he said, with the help of a local Muslim leader.

"If it hadn't been for Islam, I'd probably be dead," he told me. "Just had a negative attitude, you understand. Growing up in Altgeld, I'd soak up all the poison the white man feeds us. See, the folks you're working with got the same problem, even though they don't realize it yet. They spend half they lives worrying about what white folks think. They know what this country has done to their momma, their daddy, their sister. So the truth is they hate white folks, but they can't admit it to themselves. Keep it all bottled up, fighting *themselves*. Waste a lot of energy that way."

That was the truth as Rafiq saw it. His loyalty was to family, mosque, and the Black race. Everyone else he mistrusted. For him, it was Black self-respect that had elected Mayor

My father, Barack Obama Sr., grew up in Kenya and studied at the University of Hawaii, where he met my mother, Ann.

My mother, Ann Dunham, was adventurous and suspicious of anyone who thought the world was easily defined. "The world is complicated, Bar," she told me. "That's why it's interesting."

Here I am as a child in Hawaii, riding my tricycle.

My maternal grandfather, Stanley Dunham, with my maternal grandmother, Madelyn Dunham. They were married just before Pearl Harbor was bombed in 1941. My grandfather served in the Army during World War II, while my grandmother worked on a bomber plane assembly line.

This is my father as a child. He's held by my paternal grandmother, Habiba Akumu Obama, my paternal grandfather's second wife. My family members say that my father took after Akumu in his wild and stubborn ways, even though he was raised mostly by my grandfather's third wife, Sarah.

Me playing with my grandfather on a beach in Hawaii. My grandfather liked to play pranks on tourists at the beach and tell them I was the great-grandson of Hawaii's first king, Kamehameaha.

My mother married Lolo Soetoro, my stepfather, when I was six. We moved to Indonesia, where he was from, and a few years later my half sister Maya was born.

Here I am sightseeing in Indonesia, before returning to live with my grandparents and finish school in Hawaii.

My father was a stranger to me when he came to visit my mother and me for Christmas one year. It was the last time I saw him in person before he died, and the photos from that visit are the only ones I have of us together.

As a young man in high school, I wore my hair long and thought I was pretty hip.

Toot, Gramps, and my mother celebrating at my high school graduation. In Hawaii, flower leis are a common gift for graduations and other celebrations.

I continued to play basketball through my senior year of high school. I loved the moments when the whole team moved as one unit, and some of my closest friendships started on the court.

After high school I moved to Los Angeles to attend Occidental College—here I am as a young student. At Occidental I met friends who changed my worldview and started getting involved in politic causes I believed in.

After Occidental, I transferred to Columbia University in New York City. Here I am in Central Park.

After I graduated from Columbia, I moved to Chicago and started working as a community organizer, attending meeting like this to learn about the needs of people in places like the Altgeld Gardens public housing project.

I first got to know my half sister Auma by writing letters to her. But when she first visited me in Chicago, we quickly fell into a close and easy relationship as siblings, though we grew up continents apart.

I left Chicago
and community
organizing to
attend Harvard
Law School,
hoping to learn
new ways to
help make real
change in the
world.

My first trip to Kenya was in
1987. Here I am with my step-
grandmother "Mama Sarah"
(below) and with Mama Sarah,
Auma, and Auma's mother,
Kezia Obama (left), outside the
family homestead in Alego.

Before we were married, Michelle joined me for a trip to the family homestead in Alego.

My siblings Roy, Maya, and Auma came to my wedding to Michelle in 1992. Michelle's brother Craig, and his the wife, Janis, joined for a family photo

Washington, just as Black self-respect had turned around the lives of drug addicts with the guidance of his Muslim brothers. Progress was within our grasp so long as we didn't betray ourselves.

But how do you define betrayal? That's what I'd been wrestling with since I'd first picked up Malcolm X's autobiography. I was convinced that the positive message of Black solidarity, self-reliance, and discipline didn't need to depend on hatred of white people. We could tell this country where it was wrong without ceasing to believe in its capacity for change.

To Rafiq, though, blaming ourselves for anything would mean accepting the explanations that some white people had always offered for Black poverty: that we were genetically inferior, that our culture was weak. He would tell people that the self-loathing they felt, what kept them drinking or thieving, was planted by white people. Rid them from your mind and find your true power liberated.

For all his professed love of Black people, though, Rafiq seemed to distrust them an awful lot. Once, after a particularly thorny meeting with the city, I asked Rafiq whether he could bring out his followers if a public showdown became necessary.

"I don't got time to run around passing out flyers trying to explain everything to the public," Rafiq said. "Most of the folks out here don't care one way or another. The ones that do are gonna be double-crossing Negroes trying to mess things up."

I disagreed with Rafiq's thinking, but I also knew the real reason for his lack of effectiveness. Neither his organization nor his mosque had more than fifty members. The reason he had influence was that he showed up at so many meetings and shouted his opponents into submission.

Rafiq's program of "Black nationalism" could thrive as an emotion—winning the applause of the unemployed teenager listening on the radio or the businessman watching late-night TV—but it floundered when it came to getting anything done.

What the Black nationalists wouldn't accept was that white people were not just phantoms to be erased from our dreams. They were part of our everyday lives. Even Black people who were sympathetic to Black nationalists had to make practical choices every day. The Black accountant had to think twice about choosing to do business at a Black-owned bank if it charged him extra for checking and couldn't afford the risk of giving him a loan. The Black nurse might say, "White folks I work with ain't so bad, and even if they were, I can't be quitting my job—who's gonna pay my rent tomorrow, or feed my children today?"

Rafiq had no ready answers to such questions; he was less interested in changing the rules of power than the color of those who had it and enjoyed its privileges. His approach was actually the very thing that Malcolm X had sought to root out: one more feeder of fantasy, one more excuse for inaction.

Fortunately, nobody I spoke with in the neighborhood seemed to take Rafiq's talk very seriously. They saw it as just that—talk. What concerned me more was the gap between our talk and our actions. Didn't self-esteem finally depend on our ability to translate words into action? It was that belief that led me into organizing, and it was that belief that would lead me to conclude that notions of purity—of race or of culture—could not be the basis for Black self-esteem.

Our sense of wholeness would have to arise from something more fine than the bloodlines we'd inherited. It would have to come from the messy, contradictory details of our own experience.

CHAPTER 10

I ran to the airport arrivals hall as fast as I could. Panting for breath, I spun around several times, my eyes scanning the crowds of Indians, Germans, Poles, Thais, and Czechs gathering their luggage.

I knew I should have left earlier! Maybe she had gotten worried and tried to call. What if she had walked right past me and I hadn't even known it?

I looked down at the photograph in my hand, the one she had sent me two months earlier, smudged now from too much handling.

Then I looked up, and the picture came to life: a Kenyan woman emerging from behind the customs gate, moving with easy, graceful steps, her bright, searching eyes fixed on my own.

"Barack?"

"Auma?"

"Oh my . . ."

I lifted my sister off the ground as we embraced, and we laughed and laughed as we looked at each other. I picked up her bag and we began to walk to the parking garage, and she slipped her arm through mine. And I knew at that moment, somehow, that I loved her naturally, easily and fiercely. Even now I can't explain it; I only know that the love was true, and still is, and I'm grateful for it.

"So, brother," Auma said as we drove into Chicago, "tell me everything."

"About what?"

"Your life, of course."

I told her about Chicago and New York, my work as an organizer, my mother and grandparents and Maya—she had heard so much about them from our father, she said, she felt as if she already knew them. She described Germany, where she was trying to finish a master's degree in linguistics.

"I have no right to complain, I suppose," she said. "I have a scholarship, an apartment. I don't know what I would be doing if I was still in Kenya. But the Germans . . . They think of themselves as very liberal when it comes to Africans, but if you scratch the surface you see they still have the attitudes of their childhood. In German fairy tales, Black people are always the goblins. Sometimes I try to imagine what it must have been like for the Old Man, leaving home for the first time. Whether he felt that same loneliness . . ."

The Old Man. That's what Auma called our father. It sounded right, at once familiar and distant, an elemental force that isn't fully understood. In my apartment, Auma held up the picture of him that sat on my bookshelf.

"He looks so innocent, doesn't he? So young." She held the picture next to my face. "You have the same mouth."

I told her she should lie down and get some rest while I went to my office.

She shook her head. "I'm not tired. Let me go with you."

"You'll feel better if you take a nap."

She said, "Agh, Barack! I see you're bossy like the Old Man. And you only met him once? It must be in the blood."

I laughed, but she didn't; instead, her eyes wandered over my face as if it were a puzzle to solve.

I gave her a tour of the South Side that afternoon, the same drive I had taken in my first days in Chicago, only with some of my own memories now. When we stopped by my office, Angela, Mona, and Shirley happened to be there. They asked Auma all about Kenya and how she braided her hair and how come she talked so pretty, like the queen of England, and the four of them enjoyed themselves thoroughly talking about me and all my strange habits.

"They seem very fond of you," Auma said afterward. "They remind me of our aunties back home." She rolled down the window and stuck her face into the wind, watching Michigan Avenue pass by: the gutted remains of a once-famous theater, a garage full of rusted cars. "Are you doing this for them, Barack?" she asked, turning back to me. "This organizing business?"

I shrugged. "For them. For me."

That same expression of puzzlement, and fear, returned to Auma's face. "I don't like politics much," she said.

"Why's that?"

"I don't know. People always end up disappointed."

There was a letter waiting for her in my mailbox when we got home; it was from the German law student she'd been dating. It was at least seven pages long, and as I prepared dinner, she sat at the kitchen table and laughed and sighed and clicked her tongue.

She told me his name was Otto and he was different from many of the Germans she met. "He's so sweet! And sometimes I treat him so badly! I don't know, Barack. Sometimes I think it's just impossible for me to trust anybody completely. I think of what the Old Man made of his life, and the idea of marriage gives me, how do you say . . . the shivers. Also, with Otto and his career, we would have to live in Germany. I imagine what it would be like, living my life as a foreigner, and I don't think I could take it."

She folded her letter and put it back in the envelope. "What about you, Barack?" she asked. "Do you have these problems, or is it just your sister who's so confused?"

"I think I know what you're feeling."

"Tell me."

"Well . . . there was a woman in New York that I loved.

She was white. She had dark hair, and specks of green in her eyes. Her voice sounded like a wind chime. We saw each other for almost a year. You know how you can fall into your own private world? Just two people, hidden and warm. Your own language. Your own customs. That's how it was.

"Anyway, one weekend she invited me to her family's country house. The parents were there, and they were very gracious. It was autumn, beautiful, with woods all around us, and we paddled a canoe across this round, icy lake with small gold leaves along the shore. The family knew every inch of the land. They knew how the hills had formed, how the glacial drifts had created the lake, the names of the earliest white settlers—their ancestors—and before that, the names of the American Indians who'd once hunted the land. The library was filled with old books and pictures of her grandfather with famous people—presidents, diplomats, industrialists. Standing in that room, I realized that our two worlds were as distant from each other as Kenya is from Germany. And I knew that if we stayed together I'd eventually live in her world. After all, I'd been living in other people's worlds most of my life. Between the two of us, I was the one who knew how to live as an outsider."

"So what happened?"

"I pushed her away and then we broke up." I shrugged. "Of course, even if she'd been more like me it still might not have worked out. There are several Black ladies who've broken my heart just as good."

"Do you ever hear from her?"

"I got a postcard at Christmas. She's happy now; she's met someone. And I have my work."

"Is that enough?"

"Sometimes."

I TOOK THE next day off so we could spend time together. But we didn't speak much about our father. It was only that night, after dinner and a long walk along the lake's crumbling break wall, that we both sensed we couldn't go any further until we opened up the subject.

I made some tea and Auma began to tell me about the Old Man, at least what she could remember. "I can't say I really knew him," she began. "Maybe nobody did . . . not really. His life was so scattered. People only knew scraps and pieces, even his own children.

"I was scared of him. He was away when I was born. In Hawaii with your mum, and then at Harvard. When he came back to Kenya, our oldest brother, Roy, and I were small children. We had lived with our mum in the country, in Alego. He came back with an American woman named Ruth, and he took us from our mother to live with them in Nairobi. Ruth was the first white person I'd ever been near, and suddenly she was supposed to be my new mother."

"Why didn't you stay with your own mother?"

Auma shook her head. "I don't know exactly. In Kenya, men get to keep children in a divorce—if they want them. I asked my mum, but it's difficult for her to talk about. She thought we would be better off living with the Old Man because he was rich.

"In those first years, the Old Man was doing really well. He was working for an American oil company. It was only a few years after Kenyan independence, and he was well connected with the top government people. He had gone to school with them. The vice president, ministers, they would come to the house. He had a big house and a big car, and everybody was impressed because he was so young and had so much education from abroad. And he had an American wife, which was still rare—although later, when he was still married to Ruth, he would go out sometimes with my real mum. As if he had to show people that he could also have this beautiful African woman whenever he chose.

"Ruth was nice enough to us then. She treated us almost like her own children. Her parents were rich, I think, and they would send us beautiful presents from the States. I'd get really excited whenever a package came from them. But then things began to change. When Ruth gave birth to Mark and David, her attention shifted to them. The Old Man left the American company to work in the government. He may have had political ambitions. But by 1966 or 1967, the divisions in Kenya had become more serious. The vice president complained that the government was becoming corrupt. There was terrible fighting between the tribes. People were being killed.

"Most of the Old Man's friends just kept quiet and learned to live with it. But the Old Man began to speak up. He would tell people that the fighting was going to ruin the country. His friends tried to warn him about saying such things in public, but he didn't care. He always thought he knew what was best, you see. Word got around that the Old Man was a troublemaker. The president called him in and told him that, because he could not keep his mouth shut, he would not work again 'until he had no shoes on his feet.'

"I don't know how much of these details are true. But I know that with the president as an enemy, things became very bad for the Old Man. He was banished from the government, and even foreign companies were told not to hire him. Finally, he had to accept a small job with the Water Department. Even this was possible only because one of his friends pitied him. The Old Man began to drink heavily, and many of the people he knew stopped coming to visit because now it was dangerous to be seen with him. They told him that maybe if he apologized, he would be all right. But he continued to say whatever was on his mind.

"I understood most of this only when I was older. At the time, I just saw that life at home became very difficult. The Old Man never spoke to Roy or myself except to scold us. He would come home very late, drunk, and I could hear him shouting at Ruth, telling her to cook him food. Ruth became very bitter at how the Old Man had changed. Sometimes, when he wasn't home, she would tell Roy and me that he was crazy. I didn't blame her—I probably agreed. But I noticed that, even more than before, she treated us differently from her own two sons. Roy and I felt like we had no one.

"She left when I was twelve or thirteen, after the Old Man had had a serious car accident. He had been drinking, I think, and the driver of the other car, a white farmer, was killed. For a long time the Old Man was in the hospital, almost a year, and Roy and I lived basically on our own. When the Old Man finally got out of the hospital, that's when he went to visit you and your mum in Hawaii. He told us that the two of you would be coming back with him and we would have a proper family. But you weren't with him when he returned, and Roy and I were left to deal with him by ourselves.

"That was a terrible time. We had no place to live and bounced from relative to relative. The Old Man had so little money, he would have to borrow from relatives just for food. This made him more ashamed, I think, and his temper got worse. He would never admit to us that anything was wrong. I think that's what hurt the most—the way he still put on airs about how we were the children of Dr. Obama. We would have empty cupboards, and he would donate money to charities just to keep up appearances!

"Finally Roy left, and I was left alone with the Old Man. Sometimes I would stay up half the night, waiting for him to come home, worrying that something terrible had happened. He would stagger in drunk and come into my room and wake me because he wanted company or something to eat. He would talk about how unhappy he was and how he had been betrayed. I would be so sleepy, I wouldn't understand anything he was saying.

"The only thing that saved me was Kenya High School. It was a very strict girls' boarding school, and when it was in session I would stay there instead of with the Old Man. The school gave me some sense of order, you see. Something to hold on to.

"One year, the Old Man couldn't even pay my school fees, and I was sent home. I was so ashamed, I cried all night. But I was lucky. One of the headmistresses gave me a scholarship that let me stay on. It's sad to say, but as much as I cared for the Old Man, I was glad not to have to live with him anymore.

"In my last two years in high school, the Old Man's situation improved. The president died, and our father got a job with the Ministry of Finance and started to have money again, and influence. But he never got over his bitterness at seeing the people he grew up with—the ones who showed more political sense—rise ahead of him. And it was too late to pick up the pieces of his family. For a long time he lived alone in a hotel room, even when he could afford again to buy a house. I almost never saw him, and when I did, he didn't know how to behave with me. We were like strangers, but he still wanted to pretend that he was a model father and could tell me how to behave.

"It was only after I got my scholarship to study in Germany that I began to let go of some of the anger I felt toward him. With distance, I could see what he had gone through, how even he had never really understood himself.

"Only at the end, after making such a mess of his life, do I think he was beginning to change. The last time I saw him, he was on a business trip, representing Kenya at a conference in Europe. I wasn't sure how things would go, because we hadn't spoken for so long. But when he arrived in Germany he seemed really relaxed, almost peaceful. We had a really good time. You know, even when he was being completely unreasonable he could be so charming! He took me to London, and we stayed in a fancy hotel, and he introduced me to all his friends at a British club. He was pulling out chairs for me and making a great fuss, telling all his friends how proud he was of me. I felt like a little girl again. Like his princess."

For some time, Auma had been staring at our father's photograph, soft-focused in the dim light. Now she stood up and went to the window, her back to me. She began to shake violently, and I came up behind her and put my arms around her as she wept.

"Do you see, Barack?" she said between sobs. "I was just starting to know him. It was just getting to the point where . . . where he might have explained himself. He might have turned the corner, found some inner peace. When he died, I felt so . . . cheated. As cheated as you must have felt."

Auma's body suddenly straightened and she wiped her eyes with her shirtsleeve. "Ah, look at what you've made your sister do," she said.

"You know, the Old Man used to talk about you so much! He would show off your picture to everybody and tell us how well you were doing in school. I guess your mum and him used to exchange letters. I think those letters really comforted him. During the really bad times, when everybody seemed to have turned against him, he would bring her letters into my room and start reading them out loud. 'You see!' he would say. 'At least there are people who truly care for me.'"

After a while, she curled up under a blanket and fell into a sound sleep. But I remained awake, looking at the stillness of her face, listening to the rhythm of her breathing, trying to make some sense out of all that she'd said. I felt as if my world had been turned upside down—as if I had woken up to find a blue sun in a yellow sky. All my life, I had carried a single image of my father, one that I had sometimes rebelled against but had never questioned: the brilliant scholar, the generous friend, the upstanding leader. Because he was not there, I'd had no reason to change that image. I'd never seen what most men see at some point in their lives: their father's body shrinking, their father's best hopes dashed, their father's face lined with grief and regret.

I'd seen weakness in other men—Gramps and his disappointments, Lolo and his compromises. I loved them and respected them for the struggles they went through, recognizing them as my own, but I never wanted to follow in their footsteps. My father was different. His voice had remained untainted, always inspiring. I imagined him with the qualities of heroic Black men like W.E.B. Du Bois or Nelson Mandela. I could almost hear him rebuking me: "You do not work hard enough, Barry. You must help in your people's struggle. Wake up, Black man!"

Now, as I sat in the glow of a single light bulb, that image had suddenly vanished. Replaced by... what? A bitter drunk? An abusive husband? A defeated, lonely bureaucrat? To think that all my life I had been wrestling with someone who didn't exist!

If Auma hadn't been in the room, I would have probably laughed out loud. The king is overthrown, I thought. The man behind the curtain isn't a wizard. I can do what I please. Whatever I do, I won't do much worse than he did. The fantasy of my father had kept me from despair. Now he was dead, truly. He could no longer tell me how to live.

All he could tell me, perhaps, was what had happened to him. What had happened to all his vigor, his promise? He hadn't been able to tell me his true feelings when he returned to Hawaii, any more than I had been able to express my ten-year-old desires. Now, I looked into Auma's sleeping face and saw the price we had paid for that silence.

TEN DAYS LATER, Auma and I sat in the hard plastic seats of the airport terminal, looking out at the planes. I asked what she was thinking about, and she smiled softly.

"I was thinking about Alego," she said. "Home Square— our grandfather's land, where Granny still lives. It's the most beautiful place, Barack. When I'm in Germany, and it's cold outside, and I'm feeling lonely, I close my eyes and imagine I'm there. Sitting in the compound, surrounded by big trees that our grandfather planted. Granny is talking, telling me something funny, and I can hear the cow swishing its tail behind us, and the chickens pecking. And under the mango tree, near the cornfields, is the place where the Old Man is buried. . . ."

Her flight was starting to board. We remained seated, and Auma closed her eyes, squeezing my hand.

"We need to go home," she said. "We need to go home, Barack, and see him there."

CHAPTER 11

One day, Mayor Harold Washington came for a visit.

He wasn't visiting me personally. He was coming to cut the ribbon for the new MET (Mayor's Office of Employment and Training) center. His presence was considered a great victory, and for weeks Rafiq had begged to have the activities start at his building. He was one of many begging for a photo op.

"You've sure become popular, Barack," said my secretary as the phone rang yet again.

I looked now at the crowd that had gathered inside Rafiq's warehouse, mostly politicians and hangers-on, all of them taking peeks out the door every few minutes while plainclothes police officers spoke into their walkie-talkies and surveyed the scene. "Remember," I told Angela, "try to get the mayor to commit to come to our rally in the fall. Tell him about all the work we're doing out here, and why—"

At that moment, a murmur ran through the crowd,

then a sudden stillness. A large motorcade pulled up, a limousine door opened, and there was the Man himself. He wore a plain blue suit and a rumpled trench coat; his gray hair looked a little frazzled, and he was shorter than I had expected. Still, he had presence, and the smile of a man at the peak of his powers. The crowd chanted—"Ha-rold! Ha-rold!"—and the mayor made a small pirouette, his hand held up in acknowledgment.

He began making his way through the throng. Past the senator and the alderman. Past Rafiq and me. Until he finally came to a stop in front of Angela.

"Ms. Rider." He took her hand and made a slight bow. "It's a pleasure. I've heard excellent things about your work."

Angela looked like she was going to pass out. The mayor offered her his arm, and together they walked toward the door, the crowd pressing behind them.

"Honey, can you believe this?" Shirley whispered to Mona.

The ceremony lasted about fifteen minutes. The mayor congratulated us on our civic involvement, while the senator and the alderman jockeyed for position behind him, smiling widely for the photographers they'd hired. The ribbon was cut, and that was it.

As the limousine sped away, the crowd scattered almost instantly, leaving just a few of us standing in the litter-blown road.

I walked over to Angela, who was busy laughing and crowing with Shirley and Mona.

"Did he agree to come to our rally?" I asked Angela.

The three of them looked at me impatiently. "What rally?"

I threw up my hands and stomped away. I was furious that she had forgotten. As I reached my car, Deacon Wilbur Milton, copresident of our organization, came up from behind. With his short, reddish beard and round cheeks, he always reminded me of Santa Claus.

"Where you off to in such a hurry?" he said.

"I don't know," I said, fuming. "Somewhere. You wanna know something, Will?"

"What?"

"We act like a bunch of starstruck children. Here we are, with a chance to show the mayor that we're real players in the city, and instead we're worrying about whether we got a picture taken with him—"

"You mean you didn't get yourself a picture?" Will smiled and held up a Polaroid shot of himself and the mayor. He put a hand on my shoulder. "You need to lighten up a little bit. What you call trifling was the most fun Angela and them have had all year. It made 'em feel important. And you made it happen. So what if they forgot to invite Harold to a rally? We can always call him back."

"I'm just frustrated."

"You want everything to happen fast. Like you got something to prove out here. You don't have to prove nothing to us, Barack. We love you, man. Jesus loves you!"

ALMOST A YEAR had passed since my arrival in Chicago, and not only had Angela, Mona, and Shirley decided not to quit, but our work was finally starting to make a difference. A street-corner group we had pulled together had fifty members who organized neighborhood cleanups, sponsored career days for youth, won agreements to improve sanitation. Run-down parks and playgrounds were overhauled, streets repaired, crime-watch programs started. And now there was a new job center where an empty storefront had been.

I began receiving invitations to sit on panels and conduct workshops; local politicians knew my name, even if they still couldn't pronounce it.

"You should have seen him when he first got here," I overheard Shirley tell a new leader one day. "He was just a boy. I swear, you look at him now, you'd think he was a different person." She spoke like a proud parent.

It should have been enough. And yet I wasn't satisfied.

Maybe it was connected to everything Auma had told me about the Old Man. Before her visit, I'd felt the need to live up to his expectations. Now I felt as if I had to make up for all his mistakes—even if I didn't know quite what they'd been.

Change, *real* change, had seemed like such an attainable goal back in college, a matter of personal will and my mother's faith. If I wanted to boost my grade-point average or drink less alcohol, it seemed like a simple matter of taking responsibility. But now, nothing seemed simple.

Who was responsible for the disorder and deterioration of a place like Altgeld? There wasn't some easily blamed cast of villainous, cigar-chomping politicians or racist sheriffs holding the neighborhood down. Those who held power in Altgeld were paid managers or members of the tenant council—a small band of older Black men and women, all of them bone-weary. Most of them did not mean badly, but they were fearful, sometimes greedy for power and perks. The people in the neighborhood included teachers, drug counselors, and police officers. Some were there only for the paycheck; others sincerely wanted to help, but they had lost confidence in their ability to keep the world around them from slowly falling apart. With that loss of confidence came a loss in the capacity for outrage. And so the idea of responsibility—their own and that of others—was gradually replaced by cynical humor and low expectations.

So I did feel that there was something to prove—that what I did counted for something, that I wasn't a fool chasing pipe dreams.

IT WAS DR. MARTHA Collier who eventually lifted me out my funk. She was the principal of Carver Elementary, one of the two elementary schools in Altgeld. The day I met her, a girl was coming out her office.

"She's the mother of one of our kids," Dr. Collier told me. "A junkie. Her boyfriend was arrested last night and can't make bail. So tell me—what can your organization do for someone like her?"

"I was hoping *you'd* have some suggestions," I said.

"Short of tearing this whole place down and giving people a chance to start over, I'm not sure."

She had been a teacher for two decades and a principal for ten years, and had fought to set up a center that brought teenage parents into the classroom to learn with their children.

"Most of the parents here want what's best for their child," Dr. Collier explained. "They just don't know how to provide it. So we counsel them on nutrition, health care, how to handle stress. We teach the ones who need it to read so they can read to their child at home. What we can't do is change the environment these girls and their babies go back to every day."

As she showed me out, I saw a wobbly line of five- and six-year-olds. How happy and curious and trusting they all seemed, despite the rocky way they'd come into the world— poor, often with no fathers around, their mothers too young or addicted to drugs.

"Beautiful, aren't they?" Dr. Collier said. "The change comes later."

"What change?"

"When their eyes stop laughing. When they shut off something inside."

I began spending several hours a week with those

children and their parents. The mothers were all in their late teens or early twenties; most had spent their lives in Altgeld, raised by teenage mothers themselves. They told me about getting pregnant at fourteen or fifteen, dropping out of school, rarely seeing their fathers. They told me about the waiting: to see the social worker, to cash welfare checks, for the bus that would take them to the nearest supermarket, five miles away, just to buy diapers on sale.

They weren't cynical, though; that surprised me. They still had ambitions. One girl, Linda Lowry, showed me an album full of clippings from a house-and-garden magazine, full of bright white kitchens and hardwood floors. She and her sister, Bernadette, told me they would have such a home one day. Bernadette's son would take swimming lessons; Linda's daughter would take ballet.

Sometimes, listening to such innocent dreams, I would find myself fighting off the urge to gather up these girls and their babies in my arms, to hold them all tight and never let go. Meanwhile, they would smile at me and ask why I wasn't married.

"Haven't found the right woman, I guess," I would say.

And they would laugh. I must have seemed as innocent to them as they seemed to me.

My plan for the parents was simple. We didn't have the power to create jobs or bring a lot more money into the schools. But we could try to get the toilets fixed, the heaters working, the windows repaired. A few victories and maybe the tenants would be inspired to form their own organization.

Then we found out about the asbestos.

Asbestos is a mineral—actually a set of six minerals—that can be extremely dangerous to inhale. But for a long time people didn't know that, and so for more than a century asbestos fibers were used to insulate homes—to keep heat from escaping and sound from getting in. Eventually, scientists proved that people were getting cancer and other health problems from breathing asbestos, and so in 1989 the U.S. Environmental Protection Agency banned most uses of it.

The trouble was, there was still plenty of asbestos in old buildings, and one of those buildings turned out to be in Altgeld. The tenants would never have known except that a woman named Sadie Evans, one of the parents, saw a tiny notice in the local paper advertising for contractors to remove asbestos from Altgeld's management office.

Sadie was a slight woman with a squeaky voice that made her seem painfully shy. But when no one else volunteered, she agreed to come with me to the office of Mr. Anderson, who managed the buildings. It was clear he was surprised to see us. She thanked him for seeing us on such short notice, then pulled out the newspaper clipping and set it on his desk.

"This is nothing to worry about, Mrs. Evans," he said. "We're doing renovation on this building, and after the contractors tore up one of the walls, they found asbestos on the pipes. It's just being removed as a precautionary measure."

Sadie asked, "Shouldn't the same precautionary measures be taken in our apartments? I mean, isn't there asbestos there, too?"

"No," he said. "We've tested them thoroughly."

"Well, that's a relief," Sadie said. "Thank you."

She shook Mr. Anderson's hand and started for the door. Then she turned back.

"Oh, I'm sorry," she said. "I forgot to ask you something. The other parents . . . well, they'd like to see a copy of these tests you took. The results, I mean. You know, just so we can make everybody feel their kids are safe."

"I . . . The records are all at the downtown office," Mr. Anderson stammered. "Filed away, you understand."

"Do you think you can get us a copy by next week?"

"Yes, well . . . of course. I'll see what I can do. Next week."

When we got outside, I told Sadie she had done well.

"Do you think he's telling the truth?"

"We'll find out soon enough."

Two weeks passed, and Sadie's calls went unreturned. So did our calls and letters to the Chicago Housing Authority (CHA).

"What do we do now?" Bernadette asked.

"We go downtown," I said. "If they won't come to us, we'll go to them."

The next day we planned our action. We wrote again to the CHA director, informing him that we would appear at his office in two days to demand an answer to the asbestos question. We issued a short press release. Children were sent home with a flyer pinned to their jackets urging parents to join us. Bernadette and Linda made calls.

But when the day arrived, I counted only eight heads in the yellow bus parked in front of the school, along with some children. Parents told us they had doctors' appointments or couldn't find babysitters. Some didn't bother with excuses, walking past us as if we were panhandlers. Everyone looked depressed.

"I guess this is it," I said to Dr. Collier.

"Better than I expected," she said. "Obama's Army."

Once the bus was rolling, I walked to the front. "Listen up, everybody! We're going to go over the script to make sure we've got it straight. What do we want?"

"A meeting with the director!" the passengers yelled.

"Where?"

"In Altgeld!"

"What if they say they'll give us an answer later?"

"We want an answer now!"

The CHA office was in a stout gray building in the center of the city. We filed off the bus, entered the lobby, and mashed onto the elevator. On the fourth floor, a receptionist sat behind an imposing desk.

"Can I help you?" she said, barely glancing up from her magazine.

"We'd like to see the director, please," Sadie said.

"Do you have an appointment?"

"He knows we're coming," I said.

"Well, he's not in the office right now."

Sadie said, "Could you please check with his deputy?"

The receptionist looked up with an icy stare, but we stood our ground. "Have a seat," she said finally.

The parents sat down, and everyone fell into silence. The children giggled. Bernadette said, "I feel like I'm waiting to see the principal."

"They build these big offices to make you feel intimidated," I said. "Just remember that this is a *public* authority. Folks who work here are responsible to you."

"Excuse me," the receptionist said. "The director will not be able to see you today. You should report any problems you have to Mr. Anderson out in Altgeld."

"Look, we've already seen Mr. Anderson," Bernadette said. "If the director's not here, we'd like to see his deputy."

"I'm sorry but that's not possible. If you don't leave right now, I'll have to call Security."

At that moment, the elevator doors opened and several TV crews came in, along with various reporters. "Is this the protest about asbestos?" one reporter asked me.

I pointed to Sadie. "She's the spokesperson."

As the TV crews set up, Sadie dragged me aside.

"I don't wanna talk in front of no cameras. I've never been on TV before."

"You'll be fine." In a few minutes the cameras were rolling, and Sadie, her voice quavering slightly, held her first press conference. As she started to answer questions, a woman in a red suit and heavy mascara rushed into the reception area. She smiled tightly and introduced herself as the director's assistant, Ms. Broadnax. "I'm so sorry that the director isn't here," she said. "If you'll just come this way, I'm sure we can clear up this whole matter."

"Is there asbestos in all CHA units?" a reporter shouted.

"Will the director meet with the parents?"

"We're interested in the best possible outcome for the residents," Ms. Broadnax shouted over her shoulder. We followed her into a large room where several gloomy officials were already seated around a conference table. Ms. Broadnax remarked on how cute the children were and offered everyone coffee and doughnuts.

"We don't need doughnuts," Linda said. "We need answers."

And that was it. Without a word from me, the parents found out that no tests had been done. They were promised on the spot that testing would start by the end of the day, and a date was set for a meeting with the director.

Out on the street, Linda insisted that I treat everybody, including the bus driver, to caramel popcorn.

"Did you see that woman's face when she saw the cameras?"

"What about her acting all nice to the kids? Just trying to cozy up to us so we wouldn't ask any questions."

"Wasn't Sadie terrific? You did us proud, Sadie."

"We're gonna be on TV!"

I tried to stop everybody from talking at once, but Mona tugged on my shirt. "Give it up, Barack." She handed me a bag of popcorn. "Eat."

As I chewed on the gooey popcorn, looking out at the lake, calm and turquoise, I couldn't recall a more contented moment.

I CHANGED IN a fundamental way as a result of that bus trip. The memory of it kept me going through all the disappointments that came later. Maybe it still does.

That evening, Sadie's face was all over the television. The press discovered that another South Side project contained pipes lined with rotting asbestos. Aldermen began calling for immediate hearings. Lawyers called.

But it was away from all that that I saw something wonderful happening. The parents began talking about ideas for future campaigns. New parents got involved. It was as though Sadie's small, honest step had tapped into a reservoir of hope, allowing people in Altgeld to reclaim a power they had had all along.

CHAPTER 12

By the spring of 1987, I had been in Chicago long enough to know that something ugly and frightening was beginning to happen to the children of the South Side.

One night I was walking with my new assistant, Johnnie, when we heard a small pop, like a balloon bursting. A boy came running around the corner, his limbs pumping wildly. He couldn't have been older than fifteen.

Johnnie dropped flat onto the grass, and I quickly followed. A few seconds later, two more boys came around the same corner, also running at full speed. One of them, short, fattish, with pants that bunched around his ankles, was waving a small pistol. Without stopping to aim, he let out three quick shots in the direction of the first boy. When he saw that his target was out of range, he slowed to a walk and stuffed the weapon under his shirt.

"Stupid m————," said the second boy. The two of them laughed. As they continued down the street, I watched their shadows on the pavement. They looked, for an instant, like regular kids, just goofing around.

The drive-by shootings, the ambulance sirens, the chalk marks where bodies had fallen—none of this was new. In places like Altgeld, fathers with prison records had sons with prison records. It was, almost literally, an inheritance passed from generation to generation. During my very first days in Chicago I had seen the groups of young men, fifteen or sixteen, hanging out on corners, their hoods up, scattering whenever police cars on the hunt for drug dealers cruised by in silence.

But there had been a change of atmosphere, like the electricity you sometimes feel in the air when a storm is approaching. There was a sense that some, if not most, of our boys were slipping beyond rescue.

Even lifelong South Siders like Johnnie noticed the change. "I ain't never seen it like this, Barack," he told me that night. He was normally full of enthusiasm, but now his round, bearded face was dark. "I mean, things were tough when I was coming up, but there were limits. In public, at home, if an adult saw you getting loud or wild, they would say something. And most of us would listen.

"Now, with the drugs, the guns—all that's disappeared. Don't take a whole lot of kids carrying a gun. Just one or two. Somebody says something to one of 'em, and—pow!— kid wastes him. Folks hear stories like that, they just stop trying to talk to these young cats out here. After a while, even the good kid starts realizing ain't nobody out here gonna look out for him. So he figures he's gonna have to look after himself. Bottom line, you got twelve-year-olds making their own rules.

"I don't know, Barack. Sometimes *I'm* afraid of 'em. You've got to be afraid of somebody who just doesn't care. Don't matter how young they are."

Back at home, I thought about Johnnie's fear, and how different it was from mine. When I wandered through Altgeld or other tough neighborhoods, my fears were always the old ones of not belonging. The idea of physical assault just never occurred to me.

I thought about Kyle, Ruby's son. He had just turned sixteen and was several inches taller than when I'd arrived two years ago, with a shadow above his upper lip, his first effort at a mustache. He was still polite to me, still willing to talk about the Bulls. But he was usually gone whenever I stopped by, or on his way out with friends. Some nights, Ruby would call me at home just to talk about him, how she never knew where he was, how his grades had continued to drop, how the door to his room was always closed.

Don't worry, I would tell her; I was a lot worse at Kyle's age. I don't think she believed that particular truth, but hearing the words seemed to make her feel better.

One day I invited Kyle to join me for a pick-up basketball game at the University of Chicago gym. He was quiet most of the ride, fending off questions with a grunt or a shrug.

I asked him if he was still thinking about the air force, and he shook his head; he'd stay in Chicago, he said, find a job and get his own place. I asked him what had changed his mind. He said that the air force would never let a Black man fly a plane.

I looked at him crossly. "Who told you that mess?"

Kyle shrugged. "Don't need somebody to tell me that. Just is, that's all."

"Man, that's the wrong attitude. You can do whatever you want if you're willing to work for it."

Kyle smirked and turned his head toward the window, his breath misting the glass. "Yeah, well . . . how many Black pilots do you know?"

On the court, Kyle's game wasn't bad, but he was guarding a guy a few years older than me, an orderly at the hospital— short but aggressive, and very quick. After a few plays, it became clear that the man had Kyle's number. He scored three baskets in a row, then started talking the usual talk.

"You can't do no better than that, boy? How you gonna let an old man like me make you look so bad?"

Kyle didn't answer, but the play between them became rough. The next time the man made his move for the basket, Kyle bumped him hard. The man threw the ball at Kyle's chest, then turned to one of his partners. "You see that? This punk can't guard me—"

Suddenly, without any warning, Kyle swung. His fist landed square on the man's jaw, dropping him to the floor.

I ran onto the court as the other players pulled Kyle away. His eyes were wide, his voice trembling as he watched the orderly struggle to his feet and spit out a wad of blood.

"I ain't no punk," Kyle muttered. And then again, "I ain't no punk."

We were lucky; somebody had called the security guard downstairs, but the orderly was too embarrassed to admit to the incident. On the drive back, I gave Kyle a long lecture about keeping his cool, about violence, about responsibility. But everything I said sounded like a cliché, and Kyle sat without answering, his eyes fixed on the road. When I was finished he turned to me and said, "Just don't tell my momma, all right?"

I thought that was a good sign. I said I wouldn't tell Ruby what had happened so long as he did, and he grudgingly agreed.

Kyle was a good kid; he still cared about something. Would that be enough to save him?

THE WEEK AFTER Johnnie and I saw the shooting, I decided it was time to go into the public schools in a big way.

They were in a state of never-ending crisis—no money, no textbooks, no toilet paper. And no one in the government seemed to care. The more I learned, the more convinced I was that better schools were the only solution for all those young men on the street. Without stable families and the promise of decent jobs that could support a family, education was their last best hope.

The people I talked to—parents, administrators—were full of excuses for why things would never get better. There wasn't enough money to do the job right, they told me—which was certainly true. The students, they said, were impossible. Lazy. Unruly. Slow. Not the children's fault, maybe, but certainly not the schools'. Maybe they aren't bad kids, Barack, but they sure have bad parents.

Those conversations, full of cynicism and hopelessness, made me angry. So Johnnie and I decided to go ahead and visit some of the area schools on our own, hoping to drum up support from parents other than the ones at Altgeld.

We started with Kyle's high school, the one in the area with the best reputation. It was a single building: bare concrete pillars, long stark corridors, windows that couldn't be opened. But it was there that we met a school counselor who made us think about the problem from a different angle. His name was Asante Moran. He was tall and imposing, his small office decorated with African themes: a map of the continent, posters of ancient kings and queens, a collection of drums and gourds. Dressed in an African print, he had an elephant-hair bracelet around one thick wrist.

"The first thing you have to realize," he told us, "is that the public school system is not about educating Black children. Inner-city schools are like holding pens—miniature jails, really. It's only when Black children start breaking out of their pens and bothering white people that society even pays any attention to the issue of whether these children are being educated."

Asante argued that a real education would start by giving a child an understanding of his or her world, his or her culture. "But for Black children, everything's turned upside down," he said. "They're learning about someone *else's* history. Someone else's culture. Not only that, this culture they're supposed to learn is the same one that's rejected them."

Asante leaned back in his chair. "Is it any wonder that the Black child loses interest in learning?"

"It's worst for the boys," he went on. "At least the girls have older women to talk to. But half the boys don't even know their own fathers. There's nobody to guide them through the process of becoming a man. And that's a recipe for disaster. Because in every society, young men are going to have violent tendencies. Either those tendencies are directed and disciplined or those tendencies destroy the young men, the society, or both."

Asante said he saw it as his job to fill the void. He exposed kids to African history, geography, artistic traditions. He tried to counteract the values of materialism and me-first individualism that they saw all around them. He taught them that Africans are a communal people, with respect for their elders.

All at once he looked at me and asked about my name.

"My father was from Kenya," I said.

He smiled. "That's where I went for my first trip to the continent," he said. "Changed my life forever. The people were so welcoming. And the land—I'd never seen anything so beautiful. It really felt like I had come home." His face glowed with the memory. "When was the last time you were back?"

I hesitated. "Actually, I've never been there."

Asante looked momentarily confused.

"Well . . . ," he said after a pause, "I'm sure that when you do make the trip, it'll change your life, too."

ON THE RIDE home, Johnnie asked why I'd never been to Kenya.

"I don't know," I said. "Maybe I'm scared of what I'll find out."

We rode in silence.

"Asante made me think about my own father," said Johnnie finally. "He drove a delivery truck for twenty years. Never seemed like he really enjoyed life, you know what I mean? On weekends, he'd just hang around the house, and some of my uncles would come over. They'd complain about what their bosses had done to 'em this week. The Man did this. The Man did that. But if one of 'em actually started talking about doing something different, or had a new idea, the rest of 'em would just tear the guy up. 'How's some no-'count nigga like you gonna start himself a business?' one of 'em'd say. They'd be laughing, but I could tell they weren't laughing inside.

"But you know, my old man never laughed when I talked about wanting to go to college. I mean, he never said anything one way or the other, but he always made sure me and my brother got up for school, that we didn't have to work, that we had a little walking-around money. The day I graduated, he showed up in a jacket and tie, and he just shook my hand. That's all . . . just shook my hand, then went back to work. . . ."

"He was there for you," I said to Johnnie.

"Yeah. I guess he was."

"You ever tell him that?"

"Naw. We're not real good at talking." Johnnie looked out the window, then turned to me. "Maybe I should, though, huh?"

OVER THE NEXT two months, Asante helped us to develop a proposal for a youth counseling network to provide at-risk teenagers with tutors and mentors, as well as reach out to their parents. It was an exciting project—which made it all the more frustrating when few of the school principals we contacted even called us back. One who did, the most enthusiastic, handed Johnnie a sheet of paper as he was leaving the man's office.

"It was a résumé," Johnnie told me. "And not just any résumé. His *wife's* résumé. Seems she's kinda bored around the house, and he thinks she'd make an 'excellent' director for our program. No pressure, you understand."

Then he reached into his briefcase and pulled out another piece of paper, waving it in the air. "Got his daughter's résumé, too! Tells me *she'd* make an 'excellent' counselor."

He began to giggle.

"Now, there's a brother with some nerve! He don't just want *one* job! He's gotta have *two*! You go in to talk about some kids, he's gonna hand you his whole *family's* résumé."

I started to laugh, too, and we both laughed until our faces were hot and our sides hurt, until tears came to our eyes, until we felt emptied out and couldn't laugh anymore. It wasn't really funny, of course. It was sad and infuriating that an educator who should be putting his students first thought more in terms of making a little extra money for his kin. But sometimes our job seemed so absurd that we had to laugh.

IT WAS AROUND this time that I decided to go to Washington, D.C., to meet my brother Roy for the first time.

Roy had married an American Peace Corps worker and moved to the States. On the phone, he described his job, his wife, his life in America as "lovely." The word rolled out of him slowly, the syllables drawn out: "Looove-leee." A visit from me would be "fan-taaas-tic." Staying with him and his wife would be "nooo prooob-lem."

My sister Auma warned me, though, that he didn't always show his true feelings. "He's like the Old Man in that way," she said.

When I arrived at the airport, Roy was nowhere to be found. I called his house and he answered, sounding apologetic.

"Listen, brother—you think maybe you can stay in a hotel tonight?"

"Why? Is something wrong?"

"Nothing serious. It's just, well, me and the wife, we had a little argument. So having you here tonight might not be so good, you understand?"

"Sure. I—"

"You call me when you find a hotel, okay? We'll meet tonight and have dinner. I'll pick you up at eight."

I checked into the cheapest room I could find and waited. At nine, I heard a knock. When I opened the door, I found a big man standing there with his hands in his pockets, a grin breaking across his ebony face.

"Hey, brother," he said. "How's life?"

In the pictures I had of Roy, he was slender, dressed in *kitenge* print, with an Afro, a goatee, a mustache. The man hugging me now was much heavier, over two hundred pounds, I guessed, the flesh on his cheeks pressing out beneath a thick pair of glasses. The goatee was gone; the African shirt had been replaced by a gray sports coat, white shirt, and tie. Auma had been right, though; his resemblance to the Old Man was scary. Looking at my brother, I felt as if I were ten years old again.

"You've gained some weight," I said as we walked to his car.

Roy looked down at his generous belly and gave it a pat. "Eh, it's this fast food, man. It's everywhere. McDonald's. Burger King. You don't even have to get out of the car to have these things."

He threw back his head to laugh, a magical sound that made his whole body shake, as if he couldn't get over the wonders this new life had to offer.

It was infectious, his laugh—although I stopped laughing along when he drove twice the speed limit, almost collided with oncoming cars, and careened over a high curb.

"You always drive this way?" I shouted over the music blasting out of his speakers.

Roy smiled. "I'm not so good, eh? Mary, my wife, she's always complaining, too. Especially since the accident . . ."

"What accident?"

"Ah, it was nothing. You see I'm still here. Alive and breathing!" And again he laughed and shook his head.

Over dinner, I asked why his wife hadn't joined us. His smile evaporated.

"Ah, I think we're getting divorced," he said.

"I'm sorry."

"She says she's tired of me staying out late. She says I drink too much. She says I'm becoming just like the Old Man."

"What do you think?"

"What do I think?" He lowered his head, then looked at me somberly. "The truth is," he said, leaning his weight forward, "I don't think I really like myself. And I blame the Old Man for this."

For the next hour, he told me, as Auma had, of all the hard times: how he had left his father's house and bounced from relative to relative. After he went to the University of Nairobi, he'd gotten a job with an accounting firm and taught himself discipline. He always arrived at work early and completed his tasks no matter how late he had been out the night before. Listening to him, I felt the same admiration that I'd felt when listening to Auma. Except in Auma I had also sensed a willingness to put the past behind her—to forgive, if not necessarily forget. Roy's memories of the Old Man seemed more painful.

"Nothing was ever good enough for him," he told me. "If you came home with the second-best grades in the class, he would ask why you weren't first. 'You are an Obama,' he would say. 'You should be the best.' And then I would see him drunk, with no money, living like a beggar. I would ask myself, How can someone so smart fall so badly? Even after I was living on my own, after his death, I would try to figure out this puzzle. It was as if I couldn't escape him.

"After the Old Man died, everyone fought over his inheritance. It was crazy! The only person I trusted was David, our younger brother. That guy, let me tell you, he was okay. He looked like you a little bit, only younger . . . fifteen, sixteen. His mother, Ruth, had tried to raise him like an

American. But David, he rebelled. He didn't want to be an American. He was an African. He was an Obama.

"When David died, that was it for me. I was sure our whole family was cursed. I started drinking, fighting—I didn't care. I figured if the Old Man could die, if David could die, that I would have to die, too. Sometimes I wonder what would have happened if I had stayed in Kenya.

"But I had been seeing this American girl, Nancy, who had returned to the States, so one day I just called her and said I wanted to come. When she said yes, I bought a ticket and caught the next plane out. I didn't pack, or tell my office, or say goodbye to anyone, or anything.

"I thought I could start over. But now I know you can never start over. Not really. You think you have control, but you are like a fly in somebody else's web."

Roy took another sip from his drink, and suddenly his speech slowed, as if he'd dropped deep into another place, as if our father had taken possession of him. "I am the oldest, you see. In Luo tradition, I am now head of the household. I am responsible for you, and for Auma, and for all the younger boys. It's my responsibility to set things right. To pay the boys' school fees. To see that Auma is properly married. To build a proper house and bring the family together."

I reached across the table and touched his hand. "You don't have to do it alone, brother," I said. "We can share the load."

But it was as if he hadn't heard me. He just stared out the

window, and then, as if snapping out of a trance, he waved the waitress over.

"You want another drink?" he asked me.

"Why don't we just get the check?" I said. It was clear he'd had too much.

Roy looked at me and smiled. "I can tell you worry too much, Barack. That's my problem, as well. I think we need to learn to go with the flow. Isn't that what you say in America? *Just go with the flow. . . .*" Roy laughed again, loud enough for the people at the next table to turn around. Only the magic was gone out of it now. His laugh sounded hollow, as if it were traveling across a vast, empty distance.

I caught a flight out the next day—Roy needed to spend some time with his wife, and I didn't have the money for another night at the hotel. We had breakfast together, and he seemed in better spirits. But I couldn't rid myself of the sense that Roy was in danger somehow, and that if only I were a better brother, I could somehow prevent his fall.

THE FOLLOWING MONDAY, well past midnight, a car pulls up in front of my apartment building carrying a troop of teenage boys and a set of stereo speakers so loud that the floor of my apartment begins to shake. I've learned to ignore such disturbances—where else do they have to go? I say to myself. But my neighbors next door have just brought home their newborn child, and so I pull on some shorts and head downstairs.

As I approach the car, the voices stop, the heads within all turn my way.

"Listen, people are trying to sleep around here. Why don't y'all take it someplace else."

The four boys inside say nothing, don't even move. I feel suddenly exposed, standing in a pair of shorts on the sidewalk in the middle of the night. I can't see the faces inside the car. It is too dark to know how old they are, whether they're sober or drunk, good boys or bad. One of them could be Kyle. One of them could be Roy. One of them could be Johnnie.

One of them could be me. Standing there, I try to remember the days when I would have been sitting in a car like that, angry and desperate to prove my place in the world. Maybe I swaggered into a classroom drunk or high, knowing that my teachers would smell beer or reefer on my breath, just daring them to say something. I start picturing myself through their eyes, and I know they're probably calculating that if one them can't take me out, the four of them certainly can.

But there is a difference between them and me: The world in which I spent those difficult times was far more forgiving. I could afford to have emotions other than anger. Sadness at my elders' injured pride. Empathy toward other people.

These boys know they have no margin for error, and that knowledge has forced them to shut off the part of themselves that could feel empathy for someone else's situation. They can't allow themselves to go soft. Their unruly maleness will not be contained, as mine finally was. Their rage won't be countered by a sense of imminent danger or of guilt at disappointing the people who raised them.

As I stand there, I find myself thinking that guilt and empathy have an important role to play. They're emotions that speak to our own buried sense that an order of some sort is required and that we have a stake in it. But I suspect these boys will have to search long and hard for that order. As far as they can tell, the world regards them with fear or contempt; they see no place for themselves in it. And that suspicion terrifies me, for I now have a place in the world, a job, a schedule to follow. As much as I might tell myself otherwise, we are drifting apart, these boys and I, into different worlds, speaking a different language, living by a different code.

The engine starts, and the car screeches away. I turn back toward my apartment knowing that I've been both stupid and lucky, knowing that I am afraid after all.

CHAPTER 13

That September, I applied to law school. It was a decision that tore me up, that I went over and over a hundred times. I felt proud of what I'd helped accomplish in Chicago, yet there was so much more to do. But I was convinced that what I would learn in law school—about the ways in which businesses and banks were put together, about how government actually worked—would help me bring about *real* change. I would learn about power in all its fine details, and I would bring that knowledge back to places like this, where it was desperately needed.

Since I wouldn't hear back from those schools until January, the only person I told was Johnnie.

"I knew it!" he shouted, and slapped me on the back.

"Knew what?"

"That it was just a matter of time, Barack. Before you were outta here."

"Why'd you think that?"

Johnnie shook his head and laughed. "Because you got options, that's why. You can leave. When somebody's got a choice between Harvard and Roseland, it's only so long somebody's gonna keep on choosing Roseland. I just hope you remember your friends when you're up in that fancy office downtown."

For some reason, his laughter made me defensive. I had gone over my decision in my mind a hundred times. I insisted to him that I would be coming back to the neighborhood, that I didn't plan on being dazzled by the wealth and power that I would certainly come into contact with. Johnnie put his up hands in mock surrender.

"Man, we're just proud to see you succeed."

Why did Johnnie doubt my intentions? Was I so defensive because I doubted them, too?

I imagined my father telling himself, twenty-eight years earlier, the same story. He would go to America, the land of dreams, and bring back knowledge that he couldn't hope to gain in his homeland. But his plans, his dreams, soon turned to dust. . . .

Would the same thing happen to me?

Perhaps I would find my answers where he spent the last part of his life, in Kenya. Auma was back in Nairobi, teaching at a university for a year. Between leaving my job in Chicago and starting law school would be the ideal time for an extended visit.

Perhaps it was finally the time. . . .

THERE WERE TWO reasons that I told Johnnie I planned to leave. The first was that he was my friend. The second was that I hoped he'd be willing to stay on and take my place as lead organizer. By the time I left, our new youth program would be up and running and the money for next year's budget would have been raised. I also hoped to bring a few more churches into our fold. If there was anything left to do, it was to reach out again to Chicago's pastors and finally figure out where they would fit into our organization's future.

I started with Reverend Philips.

His church was an old building in one of the South Side's older neighborhoods. The sanctuary was dark, with several pews that had cracked and splintered; the reddish carpet gave off a musty, damp odor. And Reverend Philips himself—he was old. With the window shades drawn, only his snow-white hair was clearly visible. His voice came at me like something out of a dream.

We talked about the church. Not his church so much as *the* church, the Black church, as an institution and as an idea.

He began by telling me about the religion of enslaved Africans who, newly landed on hostile shores, once sat in circles around fires, mixing stories of their new world with the ancient rhythms of their old. Their songs told of their dreams of survival, and freedom, and hope. Reverend

Philips recalled the Southern church of his youth, a small, whitewashed wooden place built with sweat and pennies saved from sharecropping. On bright, hot Sunday mornings, he said, all the quiet terror and hurt of the previous week would melt away as people clapped and cried and shouted to the Lord in gratitude. They prayed for those same stubborn ideas their fathers and grandfathers had: survival, and freedom, and hope.

Reverend Philips spoke of his time in Chicago and the emergence of the Nation of Islam and the Black nationalists. He understood their anger. He shared it. He didn't expect he would ever entirely escape it. But through prayer, he said, he had learned to control it. And he had tried not to pass it down to his children.

He remembered thousands of churches in Chicago, from tiny storefronts to large stone edifices. Most of the large ones had been a blend of two kinds: those where people sat stiff as cadets and sang from their hymnals, and those where preachers known as charismatics shook their bodies and spoke in tongues—unintelligible words they believed came from God.

Chicago's neighborhoods were segregated by race, and Reverend Philips thought that segregation, as bad as it was, did have one blessing. Black people with more money and more education, doctors and lawyers, worshiped right next to maids and laborers. So rich and poor, learned and unlearned, could share ideas and information and values.

He wasn't sure, he said, how much longer that mixing would go on. Most of his wealthier members had moved away to tidier neighborhoods in the suburbs. They still drove back every Sunday, out of loyalty or habit. But they no longer volunteered to tutor children or visit the homes of the poor and elderly. They were scared of the neighborhood at night. He expected that once he passed on, many of those members would start new churches, as tidy as their new streets, and their link to the past would finally be broken. Their children would no longer retain the memory of that first circle of enslaved people around the fire.

Reverend Philips's voice began to trail off; he was getting tired. As I was leaving, he asked, "By the way, what church do you belong to?"

"I . . . I attend different services," I stammered.

"But you're not a member anywhere?"

"Still searching, I guess."

"Well, I can understand that. It might help your mission if you had a church home, though. It doesn't matter where, really."

Back outside, I glanced up at the small, second-story window of the church, imagining the old pastor inside, drafting his sermon for the week. Where did my faith come from? I didn't have an answer. I had learned to have faith in myself. But is faith in oneself enough?

WITH JOHNNIE NOW handling our day-to-day activities, I met with more Black ministers, hoping to convince them to join the Developing Communities Project.

It was a slow process. Most Black pastors were fiercely independent. When I reached them on the phone, they would often be suspicious. Why would this Barack Obama, with his Muslim-sounding name, want a few minutes of their time?

Once I met them face to face, though, I would usually come away impressed. Most turned out to be thoughtful, hard-working men, with a confidence and certainty of purpose that made them by far the best organizers in the neighborhood. They were generous with their time and surprisingly willing to tell me about their own troubled pasts. One minister said he'd once had a gambling addiction. Another told me about his years as a successful executive who drank in secret. They all mentioned periods of religious doubt. That was the source of their new confidence, they insisted. They had fallen and found redemption. It was what gave them the authority to preach.

Many of the younger ministers told me about a man they saw as a mentor, the Reverend Jeremiah Wright, Jr., and toward the end of October I finally got a chance to pay him a visit. I had expected that his church, Trinity, would be imposing, but it turned out to be a modest structure surrounded with evergreens and sculpted shrubs and a small sign spiked into the grass—FREE SOUTH AFRICA. The South African system of apartheid—similar to the segregation in the American South before the civil rights movement—was still going strong at the time, and African American churches were leading the movement to pressure American companies doing business with South Africa to finally bring that hated way of life to an end.

Inside, the church was cool and murmured with activity. A group of small children waited to be picked up from day care. A crew of teenage girls passed by, dressed in brightly colored costumes for what looked like an African dance class. Four elderly women emerged from the sanctuary, and one of them shouted "God is good!" causing the others to respond giddily "All the time!"

Reverend Wright was in his late forties, with silver hair and a silver mustache and goatee. He was dressed in a gray three-piece suit. He told me he had grown up in Philadelphia, the son of a Baptist minister. At first, he didn't want to follow in his father's footsteps. After college, he served in the Marines. In the 1960s, he explored Islam and Black nationalism. But the call of his faith was a steady tug on his heart. Eventually he spent six years in a university, studying for a Ph.D. in the history of religion. He then brought everything he'd learned to Trinity United Church of Christ. His wide-ranging background, it was clear, helped him bring together the many different strands of Black experience.

Reconciling those experiences had been a challenge, but his efforts had paid off: the church had grown from two hundred to four thousand members during his two decades there. He was especially pleased that he'd managed to get more men involved.

"Nothing's harder than reaching young brothers like yourself," Reverend Wright said. "They tell themselves church is a woman's thing—that it's a sign of weakness for a man to admit that he's got spiritual needs."

On my way out, I picked up a copy of Trinity's brochure. Reverend Wright had written a list of guiding principles, and one of them warned of the dangers of chasing a certain kind of middle-class life. He warned that Black people blessed with the talent or good fortune to achieve success had to be careful not to think they were better than the rest and lose touch with their own people.

Although most of the church's members were teachers and secretaries and government workers, there was also a large number of Black professionals: engineers, doctors, accountants, and corporate managers. Many of them had worshipped in other churches or stopped going to church altogether. With successful careers in largely white institutions, they'd stopped caring about their religious heritage. But at some point, they would later tell me, they began to feel they'd reached a spiritual dead end. They felt as if they'd been cut off from themselves. In Trinity, they found something they never could get from a paycheck: an assurance, as their hair began to gray, that they belonged to a larger community, something that would outlast their own lives. The fate of the professional became bound to that of the teenage mother or the former gang member. It was a powerful program, this cultural community. It was more flexible than Black nationalism, more sustaining than my own brand of organizing.

Still, I couldn't help wondering whether it would be enough to keep more people from leaving the city or young men out of jail. Would the Christian fellowship between a Black school administrator, say, and a Black school parent change the way the schools were run? Would it reform public housing? And if men like Reverend Wright failed to take a stand, if churches like Trinity refused to engage with real power and risk genuine conflict, then what chance would there be of holding the larger community intact?

Sometimes I would pose such questions to the people I met through Reverend Wright. Maybe, they said, if you joined the church you could help us start a community program. You have some good ideas, they would tell me. Why don't you come by on Sunday? But I'd always shrug off the invitation. I believed in the sincerity of their faith, but I was still not sure of my own.

THE DAY BEFORE Thanksgiving, Harold Washington died.

It occurred without warning. Only a few months earlier, he had been reelected as mayor of Chicago, easily beating his white opponents. He had run a cautious campaign this time, without the passion he'd had the first time around. The business community had sent him their checks, resigned to his powerful presence. Some Black people had argued that he'd given up on them to win over white and Latino voters. Harold didn't pay such critics much attention. He saw no reason to take big risks, no reason to hurry. He said he'd be mayor for the next twenty years.

And then death: sudden, simple, final, almost ridiculous in its ordinariness, the heart attack of an overweight man.

It rained that weekend, cold and steady. In the neighborhood, the streets were silent. Indoors and outside, people cried. The Black radio stations replayed Harold's speeches. At City Hall, the lines stretched for blocks as mourners visited the body, lying in state. Everywhere Black people appeared dazed, stricken, uncertain of direction, frightened of the future.

In spite of their shock, those loyal to Washington began to regroup, trying to decide on a strategy for maintaining control, trying to select Harold's rightful heir. But it was too late. There was no political organization in place, no clearly defined principles to follow. Black Chicago politics had centered on one radiant individual. Now that he was gone, no one could agree on what he had stood for.

The day city council was to select a new mayor to serve until the special election, people, mostly Black, gathered outside the city council's chambers in the late afternoon, hoping for a fair and transparent process when it came to choosing Washington's successor. They chanted and stomped and swore never to leave. But in the end, the Black politicians cut deals with the white politicians and outlasted those crowds. Old-guard and conservative politicians met in secret just after four in the morning in the parking lot of a closed restaurant to nominate a soft-spoken Black alderman who would go on to let Washington's programs die with him.

I felt as if Harold Washington had died a second time that night.

IN FEBRUARY, I received an acceptance from Harvard Law School. The letter came with a thick packet of information. It reminded me of the packet I'd received from Punahou fourteen years earlier. I remembered how Gramps had stayed up the whole night reading from the school's catalog, how he'd told me I would make contacts that would last a lifetime, that I would move in charmed circles and have all the opportunities he'd never had. And I had smiled back at him, pretending to understand but actually wishing I was still in Indonesia running barefoot along a paddy field, with my feet sinking in the cool, wet mud.

I felt something like that now.

I had scheduled a luncheon that week at our office for the twenty or so ministers whose churches had agreed to join the organization. Most of the ministers we'd invited showed up, along with most of our key leadership. Together we discussed strategies for the coming year.

When we were finally finished, I announced that I would be leaving in May and that Johnnie would be taking over as director.

As it turned out, no one was surprised. They all came up to me afterward and offered their congratulations. Reverend Philips assured me I had made a wise choice. Angela and Mona said they always knew I'd amount to something. But one of our leaders, a single mom named Mary who had worked with us from the start, seemed upset. "What is it with you men? Why is it you're always in a hurry? Why is it that what you have isn't ever good enough?"

I started to say something, then gave her a hug. Mary had two daughters at home who would never know their father. Now someone else was leaving them behind.

THAT SUNDAY, I woke up at six a.m. I shaved, brushed the lint from my only suit, and arrived at Trinity Church by seven-thirty. Most of the pews were already filled, so I stuffed myself between a plump older woman who failed to scoot over and a family of four. The mother told the two young boys beside her to stop kicking each other.

"Where's God?" the toddler asked his brother.

"Shut up," the older boy replied.

"Both of you settle down right now," the mother said.

As the congregation joined in song, the deacons, then Reverend Wright, appeared beneath the large cross that hung from the rafters. The title of Reverend Wright's sermon that morning was "The Audacity of Hope." While the boys next to me doodled on their church bulletin, Reverend Wright spoke of the history of injustice, in the Bible and in more recent times. He described a painting titled *Hope*.

"It depicts a harpist," he said, "a woman who appears to be sitting atop a great mountain. Then you take a closer look and see that the woman is bruised and bloodied, dressed in tattered rags, the harp reduced to a single frayed string. Your eye is then drawn down to the valley below, where people are starving and dying from war."

"Daily," he cried, "we all face rejection and despair! And yet consider that painting, *Hope*. That harpist is looking upwards, a few faint notes floating upwards toward the heavens. She dares to hope. . . . She has the audacity . . . to make music . . . and praise God . . . on the one string . . . she has left!"

People began to shout, to rise from their seats and clap and cry out.

And I began to hear all the voices from the past three years. The courage and fear of women like Ruby. The race pride and anger of men like Rafiq. The desire to let go, the desire to escape, the desire to give oneself up to a God that could somehow put a floor on despair.

And in that single note—hope!—I heard something else. I imagined inside the thousands of churches across the city, the stories of ordinary Black people merging with the stories of David and Goliath, Moses and Pharaoh, the Christians in the lion's den. Those stories—of survival, and freedom, and hope—became our story, my story; the blood that had spilled was our blood, the tears our tears; until this Black church, on this bright day, seemed once more a vessel carrying the story of a people into future generations and into a larger world.

Yes, I had spent the last three years preaching action instead of dreams. But now I felt for the first time that the communion inside this church—even if it sometimes disguised the very real conflicts among us—could also help us to move beyond our narrow dreams, to be part of something larger than ourselves.

"The audacity of hope!" chanted Reverend Wright. "I still remember my grandmother, singing in the house, 'There's a bright side somewhere . . . don't rest till you find it. . . . The audacity of hope! Times when we couldn't pay the bills. Times when it looked like I wasn't ever going to amount to anything . . . and yet and still my momma and daddy would break into a song . . . *Thank you, Jesus. Thank you, Jesus. Thank you, Lord . . .*

"And it made no sense to me, this singing! Why were they thanking Him for all of their troubles? I'd ask myself. But see, I was only looking at the *horizontal* dimension of their lives! I didn't understand that they were talking about the *vertical* dimension! About their relationship to God above!"

As the choir lifted back up into song, as the congregation

began to applaud those who were walking to the altar to accept Reverend Wright's call, I felt a light touch on the top of my hand. The older of the two boys beside me was handing me a pocket tissue. Beside him, his mother glanced at me with a faint smile before turning back toward the altar. It was only when I thanked the boy that I felt the tears running down my cheeks.

"Oh, Jesus," I heard the older woman beside me whisper softly. "Thank you for carrying us this far."

PART THREE

KENYA

CHAPTER 14

enyatta International Airport was almost empty when my plane landed in Africa. Officials sipped at their morning tea as they checked over passports. In the baggage area, a creaky conveyor belt spat out luggage. Auma was nowhere in sight, so I took a seat on my carry-on bag. After a few minutes, a security guard approached me.

"This is your first trip to Kenya, yes?" he asked.

"That's right."

"I see." He squatted down beside me. "You are from America. You know my brother's son, perhaps. Samson Otieno. He is studying engineering in Texas."

I told him that I'd never been to Texas and so hadn't had the opportunity to meet his nephew, which disappointed him. By this time, the last of the other passengers on my flight had left the terminal. I asked the guard if any more bags were coming.

"I don't think so," he said, "but if you will just wait here, I will find someone who can help you."

He disappeared around a narrow corridor, and I stood up to stretch my back. I had imagined a more earthshaking homecoming: clouds lifting, old demons fleeing, the spirits of my ancestors rising up in celebration. A pilgrimage, Asante had called it. For folks back in Chicago, as for me, Africa had become an idea more than an actual place, a new promised land, full of ancient traditions and noble struggles and talking drums. But that was Africa from a distance—like the distance I'd had from the Old Man. What would happen when that distance was gone? What if the truth only disappointed, and my father's death meant nothing, and his leaving me behind meant nothing, and the only tie that bound me to him, or to Africa, was a name and a blood type?

I felt suddenly tired and abandoned. I was about to search for a telephone when the security guard reappeared with a strikingly beautiful woman, dark brown, slender, close to six feet tall and dressed in a British Airways uniform. She introduced herself as Miss Omoro and explained that my bag had probably been sent on to Johannesburg by mistake.

As I filled out a missing-baggage form, Miss Omoro asked, "You wouldn't be related to Dr. Obama, by any chance?"

"Well, yes—he was my father."

Miss Omoro smiled sympathetically. "I'm very sorry about his passing. Your father was a close friend of my family's. He would often come to our house when I was a child."

As we talked about my visit, I found myself trying to prolong the conversation, encouraged by the fact that she'd recognized my name. That had never happened before, I realized; not in Hawaii, not in Indonesia, not in L.A. or New York or Chicago. For the first time in my life, I felt the comfort, the firmness of identity that a name might provide, how it could carry an entire history in other people's memories, so that they might nod and say knowingly, "Oh, you are so-and-so's son." No one here in Kenya would ask how to spell my name, or mispronounce it. My name belonged and so I belonged—even if I did not understand the whole web of connections.

"Barack!" I turned to see Auma jumping up and down. I rushed over to her and we laughed and hugged, as silly as the first time we'd met. A tall, brown-skinned woman was smiling beside us, and Auma turned and said, "Barack, this is our Auntie Zeituni. Our father's sister."

"Welcome home," Zeituni said, kissing me on both cheeks.

While Auma drove, the two of them began to talk at the same time, asking how my trip had been, listing all the things I had to do and people I had to see. Wide plains stretched out on either side of the road, savannah grass mostly, an occasional thorn tree against the horizon, a landscape that seemed at once ancient and alive.

Gradually the traffic thickened, and crowds began to pour out of the countryside on their way to work, the men still buttoning their flimsy shirts; the women straight-backed, their heads wrapped in bright-colored scarves. Cars meandered across lanes and roundabouts, dodging potholes, bicycles, and pedestrians, while rickety jitneys—called *matatus,* I was told—stopped without any warning to cram on more passengers.

It all seemed strangely familiar, as if I had been down that same road before. And then I remembered other mornings in Indonesia, with my mother and Lolo talking in the front seat, the same smell of burning wood and diesel, the same look on people's faces. It seemed as if they didn't expect much more than to make it through the day, maybe hoping that their luck would change, or at least hold out.

We went to drop off Zeituni at Kenya Breweries, where she worked as a computer programmer. She leaned over again to kiss me on the cheek, then wagged her finger at Auma. "You take good care of Barry, now," she said. "Make sure he doesn't get lost again."

Once we were back on the highway, I asked Auma what Zeituni had meant about my getting lost. Auma shrugged.

"It's a common expression here," she said. "Usually, it means the person hasn't seen you in a while. 'You've been lost,' they'll say. Or 'Don't get lost.'

"Sometimes it has a more serious meaning. Let's say a son or husband moves to the city, or to the West, like our Uncle Omar, in Boston. They promise to return after completing school. They say they'll send for the family once they get settled. At first they write once a week. Then it's just once a month.

Then they stop writing completely. No one sees them again. They've been lost, you see. Even if people know where they are."

AUMA'S APARTMENT WAS a small but comfortable space with French doors that let sunlight wash through the rooms. There were stacks of books everywhere, and a collage of family photographs hanging on the wall. Above her bed, there was a large poster of a Black woman, her face tilted upward toward an unfolding blossom, the words "I Have a Dream" printed below.

"So what's your dream, Auma?" I asked.

Auma laughed. "That's my biggest problem, Barack. Too many dreams. A woman with dreams always has problems."

My exhaustion from the trip must have showed, because Auma suggested that I take a nap while she went to the university to teach her class. I dropped onto the cot she'd prepared and fell asleep to the buzz of insects outside the window.

The next morning we walked into town and wandered without any destination in mind. The city center was smaller than I'd expected, with row after row of worn, whitewashed stucco from the days when Nairobi was little more than a place for the British to stay while building railroads. Alongside these buildings, a modern city had emerged, a city of high-rise offices and elegant shops, hotels with lobbies no different from those in Singapore or Atlanta.

It was an odd mix of cultures old and new. In front of a fancy car dealership, a train of Masai women passed by on the way to market, their heads shaven clean, their earlobes ringed with bright beads. At the entrance to an open-air mosque, we watched a group of bank officers carefully remove their wing-tipped shoes and bathe their feet before joining farmers and ditchdiggers in afternoon prayer.

We wandered into the old marketplace, a cavernous building that smelled of ripe fruit and a butcher shop. A passage to the rear of the building led into a maze of open-air stalls where merchants hawked fabrics, baskets, brass jewelry, and other curios. I stopped in front of one with a set of small wooden carvings. I recognized the figures as my father's long-ago gift to me: elephants, lions, drummers in traditional headdress. "They are only small things," the Old Man had said. . . .

"Come, mister," the young man minding the stall said. "A beautiful necklace for your wife."

"This is my sister."

"She is a very beautiful sister. Come, this is nice for her."

"How much?"

"Only five hundred shillings. Beautiful."

Auma frowned and said something to the man in Swahili. "He's giving you the *wazungu* price," she explained. "The white man's price."

The young man smiled. "I'm very sorry, sister," he said. "For a Kenyan, the price is three hundred only."

Inside the stall, an old woman who was stringing glass beads pointed at me and said something that made Auma smile.

"What'd she say?"

"She says that you look like an American to her."

"Tell her I'm Luo," I said, beating my chest.

Across from us, a woman wove colored straw into baskets and a man cut cowhide into long strips to be used for purse straps. I watched those nimble hands stitch and cut and weave, and began to imagine an unchanging rhythm of days, lived on firm soil where you could wake up each morning and know that today would be the same as yesterday, where you saw how the things that you used had been made and could recite the lives of those who had made them. And all of this happened while a steady procession of Black faces passed before your eyes, the round faces of babies and the chipped, worn faces of the old; beautiful faces that made me understand the transformation that Asante and other Black Americans said they'd undergone after their first visit to Africa.

Here in Africa, you could experience the freedom that comes from not feeling watched, the freedom of believing that your hair grows as it's supposed to grow and that your rump sways the way a rump is supposed to sway. Here the world was Black, and so you were just you; you could discover all those things that were unique to your life without being accused of betrayal or living a lie.

We turned onto Kimathi Street, named after one of the

leaders of the Mau-Mau rebellion: eight years, from 1952 to 1960, when ethnic groups rose up and fought the colonialist British rulers. They lost in the end, and Kimathi was captured and executed. But they inspired Africans in other countries to mount similar rebellions. And their efforts led, in a roundabout way, to Kenya's independence in 1963.

The first prime minister and president of Kenya was Jomo Kenyatta, who would later make it impossible for my father to work. When he came into office, he immediately assured white people who were busy packing their bags that they shouldn't worry about the government taking their businesses or land. Kenya became a model of stability to Europeans and Americans, unlike its neighbors Uganda and Tanzania. Former freedom fighters put away their guns and returned to their villages or ran for government offices.

And Kimathi became just a name on a street sign for tourists to walk past.

I studied these tourists as Auma and I sat down for lunch in an outdoor café. They were everywhere—Germans, Japanese, British, Americans—taking pictures, fending off street peddlers, many of them dressed in safari suits like actors on a movie set.

A white American family sat down a few tables away from us. Two of the Kenyan waiters immediately sprang into action, both of them smiling from one ear to the other. Since Auma and I hadn't yet been served, I began to wave at the two waiters who remained by the kitchen, thinking they must have somehow failed to see us. For some time they managed to avoid my glance, but eventually an older man with sleepy eyes brought over two menus. His manner was resentful, though, and after several more minutes he showed no sign of ever coming back. At this point, the Americans had already received their food and we still had no place settings. Auma stood up.

"Let's go."

She started heading for the exit, then suddenly turned and walked back to the waiter, who was watching us with an impassive stare.

"You should be ashamed of yourself," Auma said to him, her voice shaking. "You should be ashamed."

The waiter replied brusquely in Swahili.

"I don't care how many mouths you have to feed, you cannot treat your own people like dogs."

Auma snapped open her purse and took out a crumpled hundred-shilling note. "You see!" she shouted. "I can pay for my own damn food."

She threw the note to the ground, then marched out onto the street.

For several minutes we wandered without apparent direction, until I finally suggested we sit down on a bench beside the central post office.

"You okay?" I asked her.

She nodded. "That was stupid, throwing away money like that."

We watched the traffic pass. "You know," she said eventually, "I can't go to a club in any of these hotels if I'm with another African woman. The security people will turn us away, thinking we are prostitutes. The same in any of these big office buildings. If you don't work there, and you are African, they will stop you. But if you're with a German friend, they're all smiles. 'Good evening, miss,' they'll say. 'How are you tonight?'"

I told Auma she was being too hard on the Kenyans, that it was the same in many countries where foreign businessmen and tourists had more money than the people who grew up there. But my words did nothing to soothe her bitterness. She was right, I suspected, in one way. Not all the tourists in Nairobi had come for safaris. Some were there to relive an era when white people from foreign lands could come and be served by Black people without fear or guilt.

Did the waiter who ignored us know that Black rule had come to Kenya? Did it mean anything to him? Maybe once. But then he looked around and saw his unlucky countrymen drifting into hustles and odd jobs, some of them going under. He realized he needed to support himself, and if that meant treating others better than his own people, so be it.

Then again, maybe he was torn between two worlds, remembering the hush of a village night or the sound of his mother grinding corn under a stone pallet. And so he was uncertain in each world, always off balance, playing whichever game it took to keep from losing what he had.

THAT EVENING, WE drove east to Kariako, a sprawling apartment complex surrounded by dirt lots. The moon had dropped behind thick clouds, and a light drizzle had begun to fall. At the top of three flights, Auma pushed against a door that was slightly ajar.

"Barry! You've finally come!"

A short, stocky woman with a cheerful brown face gave me a tight squeeze around the waist. Behind her were fifteen or so people smiling and waving like a crowd at a parade. The short woman looked up at me and frowned.

"You don't remember me, do you?"

"I . . ."

"I'm your Aunt Jane. It is me that called you when your father died."

She smiled and took me by the hand. "Come. You must meet everybody here. Zeituni you have already met. This . . . ," she said, leading me to a handsome older woman in a green patterned dress, "this is my sister, Kezia. She is mother to Auma and to Roy Obama."

Kezia took my hand and said my name together with a few words of Swahili.

"She says her other son has finally come home," Jane said.

"My son," Kezia repeated in English, nodding and pulling me into a hug. "My son has come home."

We continued around the room, shaking hands with

aunts, cousins, nephews, and nieces. Everyone greeted me with cheerful curiosity but very little awkwardness, as if meeting a relative for the first time was an everyday occurrence. I had a bag of chocolates for the children, and they gathered around me with polite stares as the adults tried to explain who I was.

A young man, sixteen or seventeen, stood against the wall with a watchful expression.

"That's one of your brothers," Auma said to me. "Bernard."

We shook hands, studying each other's faces. I found myself at a loss for words but managed to ask him how he had been.

"Fine, I guess," he answered softly, which brought a round of laughter from everyone.

Jane pushed me toward a small table set with bowls of goat curry, fried fish, collard greens, and rice. As we ate, people asked about everyone back in Hawaii, and I tried to describe my life in Chicago and my work as an organizer. They nodded politely but seemed a bit puzzled, so I mentioned that I'd be studying law at Harvard in the fall.

"Ah, this is good, Barry," Jane said as she sucked on a bone from the curry. "Your father studied at this school, Harvard. You will make us all proud, just like him. You see, Bernard, you must study hard like your brother."

"Bernard thinks he's going to be a football star," Zeituni said.

I turned to Bernard. "Is that right, Bernard?"

"No," he said, uncomfortable that he'd attracted attention. "I used to play, that's all."

"Maybe we can play sometime," I said.

He shook his head. "I like to play basketball now. Like Magic Johnson."

I went with Auma to see the rest of the apartment, which consisted of two bedrooms, both jammed from one end to the other with old mattresses.

"How many people live here?" I asked.

"I'm not sure right now," Auma said. "It always changes. Jane doesn't know how to say no to anybody, so any relative who moves to the city or loses a job ends up here. Sometimes they stay a long time. Or they leave their children here. The Old Man and my mum left Bernard here a lot. Jane practically raised him."

"Can she afford it?"

"Not really. She has a job as a telephone operator, which doesn't pay so much. She doesn't complain, though. She wasn't able to have her own children, so she looks after others'."

We returned to the living room, and I sank down into an old sofa and let my eyes wander over the scene—the worn furniture, the two-year-old calendar, the fading photographs. It was just like the apartments in Altgeld, I realized. The same chain of mothers and daughters and children. The same noise of gossip and TV. The same cooking and cleaning. The same hurts large and small. The same absence of men.

We said our good-byes around ten, promising to visit each and every relative in turn. As we walked to the door, Jane pulled us aside and lowered her voice. "You need to take Barry to see your Aunt Sarah," she whispered to Auma.

And then she said to me: "Sarah is your father's older sister. She wants to see you very badly."

"Of course," I said. "But why wasn't she here tonight? Does she live far away?"

"I'll explain it to you in the car," whispered Auma.

In the car, she filled me in. "You *should* go see Sarah. But I won't go with you. It's this business with the Old Man's estate. Sarah is one of the people who has disputed his will. She's been telling people that Roy, Bernard, myself—that none of us are the Old Man's children."

She sighed. "I don't know. A part of me sympathizes with her. She's had a hard life. She never had the chances the Old Man had to study or go abroad. It made her very bitter. She thinks that somehow we are to blame."

"But how much could the Old Man's estate be worth?"

"Not much. Maybe a small government pension. A piece of worthless land. I try to stay out of it. Whatever is there has probably been spent on lawyers by now. But everyone expected so much from the Old Man. He made them think that he had everything, even when he had nothing. So now, instead of getting on with their lives, they just argue among themselves, thinking that the Old Man is going to rescue them from his grave."

Then she told me about Bernard. "He's really smart. But he sits around all day doing nothing. He dropped out of school and doesn't have much prospect for finding work."

"Maybe I can help," I said.

"You can talk to him. But now that you're here, coming from America, you're part of the inheritance, you see. That's why Sarah wants to see you so much. She thinks I'm hiding you from her because you're the one with everything."

The rain had started up again as we parked the car. "The whole thing gets me so tired, Barack," she said softly. "You wouldn't believe how much I missed Kenya when I was in Germany. I thought how I never feel lonely here, where family is everywhere, nobody sends their parents to an old people's home or leaves their children with strangers. Then I'm here and everyone is asking me for help, and I feel like they are all just grabbing at me and I'm going to sink. I feel guilty because I was luckier than them. I went to a university. I can get a job. But what can I do, Barack? I'm only one person."

I took Auma's hand and we remained in the car, listening to the rain. "You asked me what my dream was," she said finally. "Sometimes I have this dream that I will build a beautiful house on our grandfather's land. A big house where we can all stay and bring our families. We could plant fruit trees like our grandfather, and our children would really know the land and speak Luo and learn our ways from the old people."

"We can do all that, Auma."

She shook her head. "Yes, but who would take care of the house if I'm not here? Who can I count on to make sure a leak gets fixed or a fence gets mended? Then I get mad at the Old Man because he didn't build this house for us. We are the children, Barack. Why do we have to take care of everyone?"

"It sounds lonely."

"Oh, I know, Barack. That's why I keep coming home. That's why I'm still dreaming."

CHAPTER 15

ernard rang the doorbell at ten o'clock sharp. He wore faded blue shorts and a T-shirt several sizes too small; in his hands was a bald orange basketball, held out like an offering.

"Ready?" he asked.

"Almost. Give me a second to put on my shoes."

He followed me into the apartment and stepped over to the desk where I had been working. "You've been reading again, Barry," he said, shaking his head. "Your woman will get bored with you, always spending time with books."

I sat down to tie my sneakers. "I've been told."

He tossed the ball into the air. "Me, I'm not so interested in books. I'm a man of action. Like Rambo."

I smiled. "Okay, Rambo," I said, standing up and opening the door. "Let's see how you do running down to the courts."

Bernard looked at me doubtfully. "The courts are far away. Where's the car?"

"Auma took it to work." I went out onto the veranda and started stretching. "Anyway, she told me it's just a mile. Good for warming up those young legs of yours."

He followed me halfheartedly through a few stretching exercises before we started up the graveled driveway onto the main road. It was a perfect day, the sun cut with a steady breeze, the road empty except for a distant woman, walking with a basket of kindling on top of her head. After less than a quarter of a mile, Bernard stopped dead in his tracks, beads of sweat on his forehead.

"I'm warmed up, Barry," he said, gulping for air. "I think now we should walk."

The courts were on the campus of the University of Nairobi, above the athletic field, their pebbled asphalt cracked with weeds. I watched Bernard as we took turns shooting, and thought about what a generous and easy companion he'd been these last few days, taking it upon himself to guide me through the city while Auma was busy grading exams. He would clutch my hand protectively as we made our way through the crowded streets, infinitely patient whenever I stopped to look at a building or read a sign that he passed by every day.

His innocent sweetness made him seem much younger than his seventeen years. But he was, I reminded myself, at an age where a little more independence, a sharper edge to his character, wouldn't be such a bad thing. I realized that he had time for me partly because he had nothing better to do. He was patient because he had no particular place he wanted to go. I needed to talk to him about that, as I'd promised Auma I would—a man-to-man talk. . . .

"You have seen Magic Johnson play?" Bernard asked me now, gathering himself for a shot. The ball went through the netless rim, and I passed it back to him.

"Just on TV."

Bernard nodded. "Everybody has a car in America. And a telephone."

"Most people. Not everybody."

He shot again and the ball clanged noisily off the rim. "I think it is better there," he said. "Maybe I will come to America. I can help you with your business."

"I don't have a business right now. Maybe after I finish law school—"

"It must be easy to find work."

"Not for everybody. Actually, lots of people have a tough time in the States. Black people especially."

He held the ball. "Not as bad as here."

We looked at each other, and I tried to picture the basketball courts back in the States. The sound of gunshots nearby, a guy peddling drugs in the stairwell—that was one picture. And another, equally true picture: boys laughing and playing in their suburban backyard, their mother calling them in for lunch. The two pictures collided, leaving me tongue-tied. Bernard returned to his dribbling.

When the sun became too strong, we walked to an

ice-cream parlor a few blocks from the university. Bernard ordered a chocolate sundae.

"Auma tells me that you're thinking about trade school," I said.

He nodded.

"What kind of courses are you interested in?"

"I don't know. Maybe auto mechanics."

"Have you tried to get into some sort of program?"

"No. Not really. You must pay fees."

"How old are you now, Bernard?"

"Seventeen," he said cautiously.

"You know what that means, don't you?" I said. "It means you're almost a man. Somebody with responsibilities. To your family. To yourself. What I'm trying to say is, it's time you decided on something that interested you. Could be auto mechanics. Could be something else. But whatever it is, you're gonna have to set some goals and follow through. Auma and I can help you with school fees, but we can't live your life for you. You understand?"

Bernard nodded. "I understand."

We both sat in silence for a while, watching Bernard dip his spoon in his sundae.

I imagined how hollow my words must be sounding to this brother of mine, whose only fault was having been born on the wrong side of our father's divided world. He must have been wondering why I thought my rules applied to him. All he wanted was a few tokens of our relationship—Bob Marley cassettes, maybe my basketball shoes once I was gone. So little to ask for, and yet anything else that I offered—advice, scoldings, my ambitions for him—would seem even less.

As we stepped into the street, Bernard draped his arm over my shoulder.

"It's good to have a big brother around," he said before waving good-bye and vanishing into the crowd.

WHAT IS A family? Is it just a genetic chain, parents and children? Or is it two people who choose each other—who form a partnership—with the idea that together they will establish a household? Does sharing the same memories make you family?

My own family circumstances were so complex and confusing that I'd never found a definite answer. Instead, I drew a series of circles around myself. An inner circle, where love was constant and unquestioned—almost taken for granted. Then a second circle, in which love and commitment were freely chosen. And then a circle for colleagues and acquaintances, like the cheerful gray-haired lady who rang up my groceries back in Chicago.

Finally, the circle widened to embrace a nation or a race, or a set of moral choices, and the commitments were no longer tied to a face or a name but were commitments I'd made to myself.

In Kenya, this planetary circle of mine almost immediately

collapsed. For family seemed to be everywhere: in stores, at the post office, on streets and in parks, all of them fussing and fretting over Dr. Obama's long-lost son. If I mentioned that I needed a notebook or shaving cream, I could count on one of my aunts to insist that she take me to some far-off corner of Nairobi to find the best bargains, no matter how long the trip took or how inconvenient it might be.

"Ah, Barry . . . what is more important than helping my brother's son?"

If a cousin discovered that Auma had left me on my own, he might walk two miles to her apartment on the off chance that I was there and needed company.

"Ah, Barry, why didn't you call on me? Come, I will take you to meet some of my friends."

And in the evenings, well, Auma and I simply surrendered ourselves to the endless invitations that came our way from uncles, nephews, second cousins, or cousins once removed, all of whom demanded, at the risk of insult, that we sit down for a meal, no matter what time it happened to be or how many meals we had already eaten.

"Ah, Barry . . . we may not have much in Kenya—but so long as you are here, you will always have something to eat!"

At first I was grateful for all this attention. I had always thought life in Africa might be this way. Yes, there was less modern technology, and it was harder to get from one place to another, but the joy of human warmth was all around me. It struck me as very different from American life, where people were so often isolated.

As the days went by, though, I began to feel less joyful and more tense. Some of it had to do with what Auma had talked about that night in the car—the awareness everyone had of my good fortune, at least compared to theirs. Not that our relatives were suffering, exactly. Both Jane and Zeituni had steady jobs; Kezia made do selling cloth in the markets. If cash got too short, the children could be sent to stay with relatives upcountry for a time.

Still, the situation in Nairobi was tough and getting tougher. Clothes were mostly secondhand, a doctor's visit reserved for only extreme emergencies. Almost all the family's younger members were unemployed, including the two or three who had managed, against stiff competition, to graduate from one of Kenya's universities. And if Jane or Zeituni ever fell ill, if their companies ever closed or laid them off, there was no such thing as collecting unemployment or disability insurance. There was only family to help—and family members were burdened by similar hardships.

Now I was family, I reminded myself; now I had responsibilities. And for the first time in my life, I found myself thinking about money: my own lack of it, the pursuit of it, the crude but undeniable peace it could buy. A part of me wished I could live up to the image that my new relatives had of me: a corporate lawyer, an American businessman, able to turn a faucet and send the riches of the Western world raining down on them.

But of course I wasn't that person. And even in the States, wealth involved trade-offs, hours devoted to making money instead of spending time with family.

Auma was in that situation. She was working two jobs that summer. With the money she saved, she wanted not only to fix up Granny's house in Alego but also to buy a bit of land around Nairobi, something that would grow in value. She had plans, schedules, budgets, and deadlines—all the things needed in the modern world. The problem was that her schedules also meant turning down invitations to family get-togethers; her budgets meant saying no to the constant requests for money that came her way. And when this happened, she would see the looks of hurt and resentment. Her restlessness, her independence, her constant planning for the future—all of this struck the family as unnatural and . . . un-African.

It reminded me of the tensions certain children on the South Side of Chicago suffered when they took too much pleasure in doing their schoolwork—how some kids might accuse them of "acting white." And it made her feel the same guilt I expected to feel if I ever did make money and had to pass those groups of young Black men on street corners as I made my way to a downtown office. It seemed as though success always threatened to leave others behind.

Toward the end of my first week in Nairobi, Zeituni took

me to visit our other aunt, Sarah. She and my father had been raised by my grandfather's second wife—Zeituni's mother, who everyone called Granny—after their own mother, Akumu, left.

Sarah now lived in an area known as Mathare, a shantytown with miles and miles of corrugated rooftops shimmering under the sun like wet lily pads.

"How many people live there?" I asked. "Half a million?"

Zeituni shook her head. "That was last week. This week, it must be one million."

We came to a series of concrete buildings along a paved road, eight, maybe twelve stories tall, and yet strangely unfinished, the wood beams and rough cement exposed to the elements. We entered one, climbed a narrow flight of stairs, and knocked on a scuffed door. A middle-aged woman appeared, short but sturdily built, with hard, glassy eyes set in a wide, rawboned face. She took my hand and said something in Luo.

"She says she is ashamed to have her brother's son see her in such a miserable place," Zeituni translated.

We were shown into a small room, ten feet by twelve, large enough to fit a bed, a dresser, two chairs, and a sewing machine. Zeituni and I each took one of the chairs, and a young woman brought us two warm sodas. Sarah sat on the bed and leaned forward to study my face.

Auma had said that Sarah knew some English, but she spoke mostly in Luo. Even without the benefit of Zeituni's translation, I could tell that she wasn't happy.

"She wants to know why you have taken so long to visit her," Zeituni explained. "She says that she is the eldest child of your grandfather, Hussein Onyango, and that you should have come to see her first."

"Tell her I meant no disrespect," I said "Everything's been so busy since my arrival—it was hard to come sooner."

Sarah's tone became sharp. "She says that the people you stay with must be telling you lies."

"Tell her that I've heard nothing said against her."

Sarah snorted and started up again, her voice rumbling against the close walls. "She says the trial is not her fault," Zeituni said quietly. "She says that it's Kezia's doing—Auma's mum. She says that the children who claim to be Obama's are not Obama's. She says they have taken everything of his and left his true people living like beggars."

Sarah nodded, and her eyes began to smolder. "Yes, Barry," she said suddenly in English. "It is me who looks after your father when he is a small boy. My mother, Akumu, is also your father's mother. Akumu is your true grandmother, not this one you call Granny. Akumu, the woman who gives your father life—you should be helping her. And look how I live. Why don't you help us, instead of these others?"

Before I could answer, Zeituni and Sarah began to argue with each other in Luo. Eventually, Zeituni stood up and straightened her skirt. "We should go now, Barry."

I began to rise out of my chair, but Sarah took my hand in both of hers, her voice softening.

"Will you give me something? For your grandmother?"

I reached for my wallet and felt the eyes of both aunts as I counted out the money I had on me—perhaps thirty dollars' worth of shillings. I pressed them into Sarah's dry, chapped hands, and she quickly slipped the money down the front of her blouse before clutching my hand again.

"Stay here, Barry," Sarah said. "You must meet—"

"You can come back later, Barry," Zeituni said. "Let's go."

Outside, Zeituni was visibly upset. She was a proud woman, this aunt; the scene with Sarah had embarrassed her. And then, that thirty dollars—Lord knows, she could have used it herself. . . .

We walked for ten minutes before I asked Zeituni what she and Sarah had been arguing about.

"Ah, it's nothing, Barry. This is what happens to old women who have no husbands." Zeituni tried to smile, but the tension creased the corners of her mouth.

"Come on, Auntie. Tell me the truth."

Zeituni shook her head. "I don't *know* the truth. At least not all of it. Your father and Sarah were actually very similar, even though they did not always get along. She was smart like him. And independent. She used to tell me, when we were children, that she wanted to get an education so that she would not have to depend on any man. That's why she ended up married to four different husbands. The first one died, but the others she left, because they were lazy or abused her. I admire her for this. Most women in Kenya put up with anything. I did, for a long time. But Sarah also paid a price for her independence."

Zeituni wiped the sweat on her forehead with the back of her hand. "Anyway, after Sarah's first husband died, she decided that your father should support her and her child, since he had received all the education. That's why she disliked Kezia and her children. She thought Kezia was just a pretty girl who wanted to take everything."

Zeituni stopped walking and turned to me. She said, "After your father went off to live with his American wife, Ruth . . . well, he would go back to Kezia sometimes. You must understand that by tradition she was still his wife—among the Luo, men often had more than one wife. It was during such a visit that Kezia became pregnant with Abo, the brother you haven't met. The thing was, Kezia also lived with another man briefly during this time. So when she became pregnant again, with Bernard, no one was sure who—" Zeituni stopped, letting the thought finish itself.

"Does Bernard know about this?"

"Yes, he knows by now. You understand, such things made no difference to your father. He would say that they were all his children. He drove this other man away, and would give Kezia money for the children whenever he could. But once he died, there was nothing to prove that he'd accepted them."

We turned a corner onto a busier road. In front of us, a pregnant goat bleated as it scurried out of the path of an oncoming *matatu*. An old woman with her head under a faded shawl motioned to us to look at her wares: two tins of dried beans, a neat stack of tomatoes, dried fish hanging from a wire like a chain of silver coins. I gazed into the old woman's face. Who was this woman? I wondered. My grandmother? A stranger?

"Now you see what your father suffered," Zeituni said, interrupting my thoughts. "His heart was too big. He would just give to everybody who asked him. And they all asked. You know, he was one of the first in the whole district to study abroad. The people back home, they didn't even know anyone else who had ridden in an airplane. So they expected everything from him. 'Ah, Barack,' they would say, 'you are a big shot now. You should give me something.' And he couldn't say no, he was so generous. Even me he had to take care of when I became pregnant.

"He was very disappointed in me. He had wanted me to go to college. But I would not listen to him, and went off with my husband. And despite this thing, when my husband became abusive and I had to leave, no money, no job, who do you think took me in? Yes—it was him. That's why, no matter what others say, I will always be grateful to him."

Zeituni stopped, as if suddenly ill, and spat into the dust.

"When your father's luck changed," she said, "these same people he had helped, they forgot him. They laughed at him. Even family refused to have him stay in their houses. Yes, Barry! Refused! They would tell Barack it was too dangerous, since he was on bad terms with the president. I knew this hurt him, but your father never held a grudge. In fact, when he was rehabilitated and doing well again, he helped these same people who had betrayed him. He would say, 'How do you know that man does not need this small thing more than me?'"

As we began to walk, she added, "I tell you this so you will know the pressure your father was under. So you don't judge him too harshly. You must learn from his life. If you have something, then everyone will want a piece of it. So you have to draw the line somewhere. If everyone is family, no one is family. Your father, he never understood this."

A FEW DAYS after my visit to Sarah's, Auma and I ran into an acquaintance of the Old Man's outside the local bank. I could tell that Auma didn't remember his name, so I introduced myself. The man said, "My, my—you have grown so tall. How's your mother? And your brother Mark: Has he graduated from the university?"

I was confused. Did I know this person? Then Auma explained in a low voice that no, I was a different brother, Barack, who grew up in America, the child of a different mother. David had passed away. And then the awkwardness on all sides—the man nodding ("I'm sorry, I didn't know") and me standing to the side, wondering how to feel after having been mistaken for a ghost.

A few days later, Auma and I came home to find a car waiting for us outside the apartment. The driver handed Auma a note.

"It's an invitation from Ruth," Auma told me. "Her son Mark is back from America for the summer. She wants to have us over for lunch."

"Do you want to go?"

Auma shook her head, a look of disgust on her face. "Ruth knows I've been here almost six months now. She doesn't care about me. The only reason she's invited us is because she's curious about you. She wants to compare you to Mark."

"I think maybe I should go," I said quietly.

"We'll both go," Auma said.

On the way to Ruth's house, Auma explained the bad feelings between the two families. She said that Ruth's divorce from the Old Man had been very bitter. After they separated, Ruth married a Tanzanian and had Mark and David take his last name, Auma told me. "She sent them to an international school, and they were raised like foreigners. She told them that they should have nothing to do with our side of the family."

She sighed. "I don't know. Maybe because he was older, Mark came to share Ruth's attitudes and had no contact with us. But once David was a teenager, he rebelled. He told Ruth he was an African and started calling himself Obama. Sometimes he would sneak off from school to visit the Old Man and the rest of the family, which is how we got to know him. He became everybody's favorite. He was so sweet and funny, even if he was sometimes too wild.

"Ruth enrolled him in a boarding school, hoping it would settle him down. But David ended up running away. Nobody saw him for months. Then Roy bumped into him outside a rugby match. He was dirty, thin, begging money from strangers. He laughed when he saw Roy, and bragged about his life on the streets. Roy insisted David go to live with him and sent word to Ruth that her son was safe. She was relieved but also furious."

Auma sipped her tea. "That's when David died in a motorcycle accident. While he was living with Roy. His death broke everybody's heart—Roy's especially. Ruth thought we had corrupted David. Stolen her baby away. And I don't think she's ever forgiven us for it."

Ruth lived in a neighborhood of expensive homes set off by wide lawns and well-tended hedges, each one with a post manned by uniformed guards. We came to one of the more modest houses on the block and parked along the curve of a looping driveway. A white woman with a long jaw and graying hair came out of the house to meet us. Behind her was a Black man of my height and complexion with a bushy Afro and horn-rimmed glasses.

"Come in, come in," Ruth said. The four of us shook hands stiffly and entered a large living room.

"Well, here we are," Ruth said, leading us to the couch and pouring lemonade. "I must say it was quite a surprise to find out you were here, Barry. I told Mark that we just had to see how this other son of Obama's turned out. Your name is Obama, isn't it? But your mother remarried. I wonder why she had you keep your name?"

I smiled as if I hadn't understood the question. "So, Mark," I said, turning to my brother, "I hear you're at Berkeley."

"Stanford," he corrected me. His voice was deep, his accent perfectly American. "I'm in my last year of the physics program there."

"It must be tough," Auma offered.

Mark shrugged. "Not really."

"Don't be so modest, dear," Ruth said. "The things Mark studies are so complicated only a handful of people really understand it all."

She patted Mark on the hand, then turned to me. "And, Barry, I understand you'll be going to Harvard. Just like Obama. You must have gotten some of his brains. Hopefully not the rest of him, though. You know Obama was quite crazy, don't you? The drinking made it worse. Did you ever meet him? Obama, I mean?"

"Only once. When I was ten."

"Well, you were lucky, then. It probably explains why you're doing so well."

That's how the next hour passed, with Ruth alternating between stories of my father's failures and stories of Mark's accomplishments. I wanted to leave as soon as the meal was over, but Ruth suggested that Mark show us the family album while she brought out the dessert.

Together we sat on the couch, slowly thumbing through the pages. Auma and Roy, dark and skinny and tall, all legs and big eyes, holding the two smaller children protectively in their arms. The Old Man and Ruth mugging it up at a beach somewhere. The entire family dressed up for a night on the town. They were happy scenes, and all strangely familiar, as if I were glimpsing some alternative universe. They were reflections, I realized, of my own long-held fantasies, fantasies that I'd kept secret even from myself. If the Old Man had taken my mother and me back with him to Kenya, would we have looked like this? I had often wished that my mother and father, sisters and brothers, were all under one roof. Here was what might have been. The recognition of how wrong it had all turned out made me so sad that after only a few minutes I had to look away.

On the drive back, I apologized to Auma for having put her through the ordeal. She waved it off.

"It could have been worse," she said. "I feel sorry for Mark, though. He seems so alone. You know, it's not easy being a mixed child in Kenya."

I looked out the window, thinking about my mother, Toot, and Gramps, and how grateful I was to them—for who they were, and for the stories they'd told.

I turned back to Auma and said, "She still hasn't gotten over him, has she?"

"Who?"

"Ruth. She hasn't gotten over the Old Man."

Auma thought for a moment. "No, Barack. I guess she hasn't. Just like the rest of us."

THE FOLLOWING WEEK, I called Mark and suggested that we go out to lunch. He seemed hesitant, but he agreed to meet me at an Indian restaurant downtown.

He was more relaxed than he had been during our first meeting. As the meal wore on, I asked him how it felt being back for the summer.

"Fine," he said. "It's nice to see my mom and dad, of course. As for the rest of Kenya, I don't feel much of an attachment. Just another poor African country."

"You don't ever think about settling here?"

"No," he said. "I mean, there's not much work for a physicist, is there, in a country where the average person doesn't have a telephone."

I should have stopped then, but something—the certainty in his voice, maybe, or our rough resemblance—made me want to push harder. I asked, "Don't you ever feel like you might be losing something?"

Mark put down his knife and fork, and for the first time that afternoon his eyes looked straight into mine.

"I understand what you're getting at," he said flatly. "You think that somehow I'm cut off from my roots." He dropped the napkin onto his plate. "Well, you're right. At a certain point, I made a decision not to think about who my real father was. He was a drunk and showed no concern for his wife or children."

"It made you mad."

"Not mad. Just numb."

"And that doesn't bother you? Being numb, I mean?"

"Toward him, no. Other things move me. Beethoven's symphonies. Shakespeare's sonnets. I know—it's not what an African is supposed to care about. But who's to tell me what I should and shouldn't care about? Understand, I'm not ashamed of being half Kenyan. I just don't ask myself a lot of questions about what it all means. About who I *really* am."

We stood up to leave, and I insisted on paying the bill. Outside we exchanged addresses and promised to write. I doubted we would, and the dishonesty made my heart ache.

CHAPTER 16

Toward the end of my second week in Kenya, Auma and I went on a safari.

Auma wasn't thrilled with the idea. When I showed her the brochure, she made a sour face. Like most Kenyans, she saw game parks, with their guarded animals and campgrounds, as part of a colonial past. "How many Kenyans do you think can afford to go on a safari?" she asked. "Why should all that land be set aside for tourists when it could be used for farming?"

I told her she was letting other people's attitudes prevent her from seeing her own country. Eventually she gave in, but only because she took pity on me.

"If some animal ate you out there," she said, "I'd never forgive myself."

And so, at seven o'clock on a Tuesday morning, we watched a sturdily built Kikuyu driver named Francis load our bags onto the roof of a white minivan. With us were a skinny cook named Rafael, a dark-haired Italian named Mauro, and a British couple in their early forties, the Wilkersons.

We drove out of Nairobi and were soon in the countryside, passing green hills and red dirt paths and small *shambas*, or farms, surrounded by plots of wilting corn. Nobody spoke, and the silence was awkward; it made me think about how I'd come to Kenya believing I could somehow force my many worlds into a single, harmonious whole. Instead, the divisions seemed only to have multiplied. I saw them everywhere.

Among the country's forty Black ethnic groups, for example. You didn't notice the fine lines so much among Auma's friends, who were younger and college-educated. But most Kenyans had ancient loyalties. Even Jane or Zeituni said things that surprised me. "The Luo are intelligent but lazy," they'd say, or "The Kikuyu are money-grubbing but industrious."

Hearing these stereotypes, I tried to explain to my aunts the error of their ways. "It's thinking like that that holds us back," I said. "We're all part of one tribe. The Black tribe. The human tribe. Look how that thinking has led to wars in other African countries like Nigeria or Liberia."

And Zeituni would say, "You sound just like your father, Barry. He also had such ideas about people."

What she meant was that he, too, was naive; he, too, liked to argue with history. And look what had happened to him. . . .

The van came to a stop. We were in front of a small *shamba*, and our driver, Francis, asked us to stay put. A few minutes later, he emerged from the house with a young African girl, maybe twelve or thirteen, who was dressed in jeans and a neatly pressed blouse and carried a small duffel.

"Is this your daughter?" Auma asked, scooting over to make room for the girl.

"No," Francis said. "My sister's. She likes to see the animals and is always nagging me to take her along. Nobody minds, I hope."

Everyone shook their heads and smiled at the girl.

"What is your name?" the British woman, Mrs. Wilkerson, asked.

"Elizabeth," the girl whispered.

"Well, Elizabeth, you can share my tent if you like," Auma said. "My brother, I think he snores."

I made a face. "Don't listen to her," I said, and held out a package of biscuits. Elizabeth took one and nibbled neatly around its edges. Auma reached for the bag and turned to Mauro.

"Want some?" she asked.

The Italian smiled and took one, before Auma passed them around to the others.

We followed the road into cooler hills, where women walked barefoot carrying firewood and water and small boys switched at donkeys from their rickety carts. Gradually the *shambas* became less frequent, replaced by tangled bush and forest, until the trees on our left dropped away and all we could see was the wide-open sky.

"The Great Rift Valley," Francis announced.

We piled out of the van and stood at the edge of a long, steep slope looking out toward the western horizon. Hundreds of feet below, stone and savannah grass stretched out in a flat and endless plain—our destination.

To the right, a solitary mountain rose like an island in a silent sea; beyond that, a row of worn and shadowed ridges. Only two signs of a human presence were visible—a slender road and a space-satellite station, its massive white dish cupped upward toward the sky.

A few miles north, we turned off the highway. It was slow going: the potholes yawned across the road, and every so often trucks would approach from the opposite direction, forcing us onto the side of the road. Eventually, we arrived at the road we'd seen from above and began to make our way across the valley floor. The landscape was dry, mostly bush grass and scruffy thorn trees, gravel and patches of hard dark stone. We passed a solitary wildebeest feeding at the base of a tree, zebras, and a giraffe, barely visible in the distance. For almost an hour we saw no other person, until a single Masai herdsman appeared in the distance, as lean and straight as the staff that he carried, leading a herd of cattle across an empty flat.

I hadn't met many Masai people in Nairobi, although I'd read a lot about them. I knew that early in the 1900s the British had broken treaties with them, evicted them from their lands, and moved them onto reservations. At the same time, their connection to the land and fierceness in war had earned them a certain respect from the British, and so in Western minds they had become noble and romantic figures, like the Cherokee or Apache in the United States.

Two hours later, we drove through the gate leading into the preserve. And there, on the other side of a rise, I saw as beautiful a land as I'd ever seen. It swept out forever, flat plains rolling into gentle hills, supple as a lion's back, creased by forests and dotted with thorn trees. To our left, a huge herd of zebra harvested the wheat-colored grass; to our right, a troop of gazelle leaped into bush. And in the center, thousands of wildebeest, with mournful heads and humped shoulders that seemed too much for their delicate-looking legs to carry.

Francis began to inch the van through the herd, and the animals parted before us, then merged in our wake like a school of fish, their hoofs beating against the earth like a wave against the shore.

I looked over at Auma. She had her arm around Elizabeth, and the two of them were wearing the same wordless smile.

We set up camp above the banks of a winding brown stream, beneath a big fig tree filled with noisy blue starlings. As we sat down to eat Rafael's stew, Francis told us a bit about himself. He had a wife and six children living on his homestead in Kikuyuland. They tended coffee and corn, and on his days off, he did the heavier work of hoeing and planting. He enjoyed his work with the travel agency but disliked being away from his family.

"If I could, I might prefer farming full-time," he said, "but the KCU makes it impossible."

"What's the KCU?" I asked.

"The Kenyan Coffee Union. They are thieves. They control what we can plant and when we can plant it. I can only sell my coffee to them, and they sell it overseas. I know they get one hundred times what they pay to me." Francis shook his head with disgust. "It's a terrible thing when the government steals from its own people."

"You speak very freely," Auma said.

Francis shrugged. "If more people spoke up, perhaps things might change."

He looked into the fire, combing his mustache with his fingers. "I suppose it is not only the government's fault," he said after a while. "Even when things are done properly, we Kenyans don't like to pay taxes. We don't trust the idea of giving our money to someone. The poor man, he has good reason for this suspicion. But the big men who own the trucks that use the roads, they also refuse to pay their share and give up some of their profits."

I tossed a stick into the fire. "Attitudes aren't so different in America," I said.

"You are probably right," he replied. "But a rich country like America can afford to be stupid."

At that moment, two Masai men approached the fire. Francis welcomed them and explained to us that they would provide security during the night.

They were quiet, handsome men, their spears stuck into the ground before them. They cast long shadows. One of them, who said his name was Wilson, spoke Swahili, and he told us that he lived in a *boma,* or camp, a few miles to the east. Auma asked if the camp had ever been attacked by animals. Wilson grinned.

"Nothing serious," he said. "But if you have to go to the bathroom at night, you should call one of us to go with you."

I drifted away from the fire to look at the stars. It had been years since I'd seen them like this; away from the lights of the city, they were thick and round and bright as jewels. I noticed a patch of haze in the otherwise clear sky.

"I believe that's the Milky Way," Mr. Wilkerson said.

He held up his hand and traced out the constellations for me. He was a slight, soft-spoken man with round glasses. At first I had assumed that he spent his life indoors, that he was an accountant or professor. But as the day passed, I noticed that he had all sorts of practical knowledge, the kinds of things I had never got around to knowing but wished that I had. He had his tent up before I drove in my first stake, and he knew the name of every bird and every tree we saw.

I wasn't surprised, then, when he told me that he had spent his childhood in Kenya, on a tea plantation. He didn't want to talk much about the past; he said only that his family had sold the land after Kenyans had won independence and had moved back to England, where he had gone to medical school. After a few years, he had convinced his wife, a psychiatrist, to return with him to Africa. They had decided not to live in Kenya, where there was a surplus of doctors, and instead settled in Malawi, where they both had worked for the government for the past five years.

"I oversee eight doctors for an area of half a million people," he told me. "We never have enough supplies. So we can only focus on the basics, which in Africa is really what's needed anyway. People die from all sorts of preventable disease—even chicken pox." He told me how he spent many of his days—digging wells, training workers to inoculate children, giving out condoms to prevent AIDS.

I asked him why he had come back to Africa.

"It's my home, I suppose. The people, the land . . ." He took off his glasses and wiped them with a handkerchief. "It's funny. Once you've lived here for a time, the life in England seems terribly cramped. The British have so much more, but seem to enjoy things less. I felt like a foreigner there."

He turned toward the campfire, and his voice began to waver. "Perhaps I can never call this place home," he said. "My own people were responsible for too much injustice. The sins of the fathers . . . I've learned to accept that." He paused for a moment, then looked at me.

"I do love this place, though," he said before walking back to his tent.

DAWN. TO THE east, the sky lightens above a black grove of trees, first deep blue, then orange, then creamy yellow. The clouds lose their purple tint slowly, then disappear, leaving behind a single star. As we pull out of camp, we see a caravan of giraffe, their long necks like strange markings against an ancient sky.

It was like that for the rest of the day. I felt as if I were seeing through a child's eyes, the world a pop-up book. A pride of lions, yawning in the grass. Buffalo in the marshes, their horns like funny wigs, tick birds on their mud-crusted backs. Hippos in the shallow riverbeds, their pink eyes and nostrils like marbles bobbing on the water.

And most of all I noticed the stillness. At twilight, we stumbled on a tribe of hyenas feeding on the carcass of a wildebeest. In the dying orange light they looked like demon dogs, their eyes like clumps of black coal, their chins dripping with blood. Beside them, a row of vultures waited with stern, patient gazes, hopping away like hunchbacks whenever one of the hyenas got too close. It was a savage scene, and we stayed there for a long time, watching life feed on itself, the silence interrupted only by the crack of bone or the rush of wind, or the hard thump of a vulture's wings.

And I thought: This is what Creation looked like. The same stillness, the same crunching of bone. There in the dusk, over that hill, I imagined the first human stepping forward, naked and rough-skinned, clumsily grasping a chunk of flint, not yet having any words for the feelings of fear and awe evoked by the sight of the vast sky. If only all of us could remember that first common step, that first common word—that time before the Biblical tower of Babel, when humans splintered apart—and be whole again.

That night, after dinner, we spoke more with our Masai guardsmen. Wilson was part of a class of young warriors known as *moran*, who had each killed a lion to prove their manhood and had participated in many cattle raids. But he'd decided that being a *moran* was a waste of time. He had gone to Nairobi in search of work, but he had little schooling and had ended up as a security guard at a bank. The boredom drove him crazy, and eventually he had returned to the valley to marry and tend cattle. Recently one of his cattle had been killed by a lion, and he and four others had hunted the lion into the preserve, even though that was now illegal.

"How do you kill a lion?" I asked.

"Five men surround it and throw their spears," Wilson said. "The lion will choose one man to pounce on. That man, he curls under his shield while the other four finish the job."

"It sounds dangerous."

Wilson shrugged. "Usually there are only scratches. But sometimes only four men will come back."

He didn't sound like he was boasting—more like a mechanic trying to explain a difficult repair.

Maybe it was that casualness that caused Auma to ask him where the Masai thought people went after they died.

At first, Wilson didn't seem to understand the question, but eventually he smiled and began shaking his head.

"This is not a Masai belief, this life after you die," he said, almost laughing. "After you die, you are nothing. You return to the soil. That is all."

For some time, Francis had been reading a small, red-bound Bible, and Auma asked if he'd been raised a Christian.

Francis nodded. "My parents converted to Christianity before I was born."

Mauro spoke, staring into the fire. "Me, I leave the Church. Too many rules. Don't you think, Francis, that Christianity is not so good? It is a white religion, no?"

Francis placed the Bible in his lap. "Such things troubled me when I was young. But the many mistakes the missionaries made were their own, not God's. And even then, they fed people when there was a drought. Some taught children to read. In this, I believe they were doing God's work. All we can do is aspire to live like God, though we will always fall short."

Francis returned to his Bible. Beside him, Auma read a story with Elizabeth. Dr. Wilkerson sat with his knees together, mending his pants while his wife stared at the fire. I looked at the Masai and wondered what they thought of us. Their courage, their hardness, made me question my own noisy spirit. And yet, as I looked around, I saw a courage I admired just as much in Francis, and in Auma, and in the Wilkersons. Maybe it was that kind of courage that Africa most desperately needed, the courage of honest, decent people with realistic ambitions, and the determination to see those ambitions through.

The fire began to die, and one by one the others made their way to bed, until only Francis and I and the Masai remained. As I stood up, Francis began to sing a deep-voiced hymn in Kikuyu, with a melody that I vaguely recognized. I listened a while, lost in my own thoughts. Walking back to my tent, I felt I understood Francis's sorrowful song, imagining it rising upward, through the clear black night, directly to God.

CHAPTER 17

At five-thirty in the evening, our train rumbled out of the old Nairobi station heading west, toward the village where many of my grandfather's family still lived—including the last of his wives who was still alive, "Granny." My stepmother Kezia, my Great-Aunt Zeituni, and my half sister Auma were in one compartment; my half brothers Roy and Bernard and I in another. While everyone stored their suitcases, I jiggled open a window and looked out at the curve of the tracks behind us.

The railway had been the single largest engineering effort in the history of the British Empire at the time it was built—six hundred miles long, from Mombasa on the Indian Ocean to the eastern shores of Lake Victoria. The project began in 1895, the year my grandfather was born, took five years to complete, and cost the lives of several hundred Indian workers. I tried to imagine a Kenyan watching this snake of steel and black smoke passing his village for the first time. Did he look at the train with envy, imagining himself one day sitting in the car where the Englishman sat? Or did he shudder with visions of ruin and war?

"How long will it take to get to Home Square?" I asked.

"All night to Kisumu," Auma said. "We'll take a bus or *matatu* from there—another five hours, maybe."

"By the way," Roy said to me, "it's not Home *Square*. It's Home *Squared*."

"What does that mean?"

"It's something the kids in Nairobi used to say," Auma explained. "There's your ordinary house in Nairobi. And then there's your house in the country, where your people come from: your ancestral home. Even the biggest minister or businessman thinks this way. He may have a mansion in Nairobi and only a small hut in the country. But if you ask him where he is from, he will tell you that hut is his true home. So, when we were at school and wanted to tell somebody we were going to Alego, it was home twice over. Home Squared."

"For you, Barack," said Roy, "we can call it Home Cubed."

Auma smiled and leaned back in her seat, listening to the rhythm of the train. "This train brings back so many memories. You remember, Roy, how much we used to look forward to going home? It is so beautiful, Barack! Not at all like Nairobi. And Granny—she's so much fun! Oh, you will like her, Barack. She has such a good sense of humor."

"She had to have a good sense of humor," Roy said, "living with the Terror for so long."

"Who's the Terror?"

Auma said, "That's what we used to call our grandfather. Because he was so mean."

Roy laughed. "Wow, that guy was *mean*! He would make you sit at the table for dinner, and he'd serve the food on china, like an Englishman. If you said one wrong thing, or used the wrong fork—pow! He would hit you with his stick. Sometimes when he hit you, you wouldn't even know why until the next day."

Zeituni wasn't impressed by Roy's tales. "Ah, you children knew him only when he was old and weak. When he was younger, aay! I was his favorite, you know. But still, if I did something wrong, I would hide from him all day, I would be so scared! He was strict even with his guests. If they came to his house, he would kill many chickens in their honor. But if they broke custom, like washing their hands before someone who was older, he would have no hesitation in hitting them, even the adults."

"Doesn't sound like he was real popular," I said.

Zeituni shook her head. "Actually, he was well respected because he was such a good farmer. His compound in Alego was one of the biggest in the area. He could make anything grow. He had studied these techniques from the British when he worked for them as a cook."

"I didn't know he was a cook."

"He had his lands, but for a long time he was a cook for white men in Nairobi. He worked for some very important people. During the World War he served a captain in the British army."

"Maybe that's what made him so mean," said Roy, now drinking his second beer.

"I don't know," Zeituni said. "I think my father was always that way. Very strict. But fair. One day, when I was a young girl, a man came to the edge of our compound with a goat on a leash. He wanted to pass through our land, because he lived on the other side, and he didn't want to walk around. So your grandfather told this man, 'When you are alone, you are always free to pass through my land. But today you cannot pass, because your goat will eat my plants.' Well, this man would not listen. He argued for a long time with your grandfather, saying that he would be careful and that the goat would do no harm. Finally, your grandfather called me over and told me to bring his machete. He had two that he kept very, very sharp. He would rub them on a stone all day. And now your grandfather tells this man, 'I will make a bargain with you. You can pass with your goat. But if even one leaf is harmed—if even *one half* of one leaf of my plants is harmed—then I will cut down your goat.'

"Well, even though I was very young at the time, I knew that this man must be stupid, because he accepted my father's offer. We began to walk, the man and his goat in front, me and the old man following closely behind. We had walked maybe twenty steps when the goat stuck out its neck and started nibbling at a leaf. Then—Whoosh! My dad cut one side of the goat's head clean through. The goat owner was shocked, and started to cry out. 'Aaiieey! Aaiieey! What have you done now, Hussein Onyango?' And your grandfather just wiped off his machete and said, 'If I say I will do something, I must do it. Otherwise how will people know that my word is true?'"

Auma shook her head. "Can you imagine, Barack?" she said. "I swear, sometimes I think that the problems in this family all started with him. He is the only person whose opinion I think the Old Man really worried about. The only person he feared."

That night I stayed up late, thinking about our grandfather. It had all started with him, Auma had said. If I could just piece together his story, then maybe everything else would fall into place.

WE ARRIVED IN Kisumu at daybreak and walked the half mile to the bus depot. It was crowded with buses and *matatus* honking and jockeying for space. Auma boarded a sad-looking vehicle with cracked tires, then stepped back out, looking morose.

"There are no seats," she said.

"Don't worry," Roy said as our bags were hoisted up by a series of hands to the roof of the bus. "This is Africa,

Auma . . . not Europe." He turned and smiled down at the young man who was collecting fares. "You can find us some seats, eh, brother?"

The man nodded. "No problem. This bus is first-class."

An hour later, Auma was sitting on my lap, along with a basket of yams and somebody else's baby girl.

"I wonder what third-class looks like," I said, wiping baby drool off my hand.

WE MADE IT to a village called Ndori and spent the next two hours sipping on warm sodas and watching stray dogs snap at each other in the dust, until a *matatu* finally appeared to take us over the dirt road heading north. Along the way a few children without shoes waved at us, and a herd of goats ran across the road to get to a stream. Finally we stopped at a clearing. Two young men were sitting under a tree, and their faces broke into smiles as they saw us. Roy jumped out of the *matatu* to gather the two men into his arms.

"Barack," Roy said happily, "these are our uncles. This is Yusuf"—he pointed to the slightly built man with a mustache—"and this," he said, pointing to the larger, clean-shaven man, "this is our father's youngest brother, Sayid."

"Ah, we have heard many great things about this one," Sayid said, smiling at me. "Welcome, Barry."

We followed Yusuf and Sayid down a path and entered a large compound. In the middle of it was a low, rectangular house with a corrugated-iron roof and crumbling concrete walls, with flowers climbing along one side of it. Across the packed earth was a small round hut lined with earthenware pots and a few chickens pecking the ground. I could see two more huts in the yard behind the house. Beneath a tall mango tree, a pair of bony red cows looked up at us.

Home Squared.

"Eh, Obama!" A big woman with a scarf on her head strode out of the main house. Her face was smooth, with sparkling, laughing eyes. This was Granny. She hugged Auma and Roy as if she were going to wrestle them to the ground, then grabbed my hand in a hearty handshake.

"Halo!" she said, attempting English.

"Musawa!" I said in Luo.

She laughed, saying something to Auma.

"She says she has dreamed about this day, when she would finally meet this son of her son. She says you've brought her a great happiness. She says that now you have finally come home."

Granny pulled me into a hug before leading us into the house. Small windows let in little of the afternoon light, and there wasn't much furniture—a few wooden chairs, a coffee table, and a worn couch. On the walls were various family mementos, including the Old Man's Harvard diploma. There were also two yellowing photographs, the first of a tall young woman with smoldering eyes, a plump infant in her lap and a young girl standing beside her; the second of an older man in a highbacked chair. The man was dressed in a starched shirt and a large cotton cloth called a *kanga;* his legs were crossed like an Englishman's, but across his lap was what appeared to be some sort of club, its heavy head wrapped in an animal skin. He had high cheekbones and narrow eyes. Auma came up beside me.

"That's him. Our grandfather. The woman in the picture is our other grandmother, Akumu. The girl is Sarah. And the baby . . . that's the Old Man."

I studied the pictures for some time, until I noticed another picture, of a white woman with thick brown hair and slightly dreamy eyes. I asked what it was doing there and Auma relayed the question to Granny.

"She says it is a picture of one of our grandfather's wives," said Auma. "He told people that he had married her in Burma when he was in the war."

Roy laughed. "She doesn't look very Burmese, eh, Barack?"

I shook my head. She looked like my mother.

After we unpacked our bags, Roy gestured for me to follow him out into the backyard. At the edge of a neighboring cornfield, at the foot of a mango tree, I saw two long rectangles of cement jutting out of the earth. They were graves. On one was a plaque that said HUSSEIN ONYANGO OBAMA, B. 1895. D. 1979. The other was covered with yellow bathroom tiles, with a bare space on the headstone where the plaque should have been.

It was the grave of my father.

Roy bent down and brushed away a train of ants that marched along the edge.

"Six years," Roy said. "Six years, and there's still nothing to say who is buried here. I tell you now, Barack—when I die, you make sure that my name is on the grave." He shook his head slowly before heading back toward the house.

HOW CAN I explain the emotions of that day? I can summon each moment in my mind. I remember Auma and myself joining Granny at the afternoon market, full of women who sat on straw mats, their smooth brown legs sticking straight out from under wide skirts, and the nutty-sweet taste of a sugarcane stalk that one of the women put into my hand. I remember the rustle of corn leaves and the concentration on my uncles' faces as we mended a hole in the fence on one side of the property. I remember how a young boy named Godfrey chased a big black rooster through the banana and papaya trees and the look in his eyes when finally Granny grabbed the rooster and, without warning, drew her knife across the bird's neck—a look of astonishment that I remembered as my own from back when I arrived in Indonesia.

In each of these moments I felt joy, but it was more than that. I had the sense that everything I was doing carried the full weight of my life; that a circle was beginning to close, so that I might finally recognize myself as I was, here, now, in one place.

Night fell quickly in the compound. Bernard, Roy, and I went to a water tank and bathed ourselves in the open air, our soapy bodies glowing from the light of an almost full moon. After dinner, Roy left, muttering that he had some people he wanted to visit. Yusuf brought out an old transistor radio that he said had once belonged to our grandfather, and fiddled with the knob until he picked up a scratchy British newscast. A moment later, we heard a strange, low-pitched moan off in the distance.

"The night runners must be out tonight," Auma said.

"What are night runners?" I asked.

"They're like warlocks," Auma said. "Spirit men. When we were children, these people here"—she pointed at Granny and Zeituni—"would tell us stories about them to make us behave. They told us that in daylight the night runners are like ordinary men. You might pass them in the market, or even have them to your house for a meal, and never know their true natures. But at night they take on the shape of leopards and speak to all the animals. The most powerful night runners can leave their bodies and fly to faraway places. Or hex you with only a glance. If you ask our neighbors, they will tell you that there are still many night runners around here."

"Let me tell you, Barry," Zeituni said in the flickering light of the kerosene lamp, "when I was young the night runners caused people many problems. They would steal our goats and even our cattle. Only your grandfather was not afraid of them. I remember one time he heard his goats bleating in their pen, and when he went to check on them, he saw what looked like a huge leopard standing on its hind legs with a baby goat in its jaws. When it saw your grandfather, it cried out in Luo before running into the forest. Your grandfather chased it deep into the hills, but just as he was about to strike it with his machete, the night runner flew up into the trees. Luckily, it dropped the goat when it jumped, and the goat suffered only a broken leg. Your grandfather brought the goat back to the compound and I cared for it myself until it was healthy again."

We became quiet; the lamplight grew low and people drifted off to bed. Granny brought out blankets and a twin-sized cot for Bernard and me, and we arranged ourselves on the narrow bed before blowing out the lamp. My body ached from exhaustion. As I drifted off to sleep I was thinking of the yellow tiles on the Old Man's grave.

IN THE MORNING, Sayid and Yusuf gave Auma and me a tour of the lands. We followed them down a dirt path, through fields of corn and millet, along a brown stream and across more fields. In front of some huts, we saw women sorting through millet and stopped to talk to one, a middle-aged woman in a faded red dress and red sneakers with no laces. She told us she remembered our father—they had herded goats together as children. When Auma asked how life had been treating her, she shook her head slowly.

"Things have changed," she said in a flat voice. "The young men leave for the city. Only the old men, women, and children remain. All the wealth has left us." As she spoke, an old man with a rickety bicycle came up beside us, then a skinny man smelling of liquor. They, too, complained about the hardness of life and about the children who had left them behind. They asked if we could give them something to tide them over, and Auma dropped a few shillings into each of their hands.

"What's happened here, Sayid?" Auma said after we were out of earshot. "There never used to be such begging."

"You are right," he said. "I believe they have learned this thing from those in the city. People come back from Nairobi or Kisumu and tell them, 'You are poor.' So now we have this idea of poverty. We didn't have this before. My mother will never ask for anything. She has always something that she is doing. None of it brings her much money, but it is something, you see. It gives her pride. Anyone could do the same, but many people here give up."

Perhaps Sayid was right that the idea of poverty had been carried in from the city, like measles. The people we'd just met had heard that some people had indoor toilets or ate meat every day. They couldn't ignore these things any more than the children of Altgeld could ignore the fast cars and fancy homes that flashed across their television sets.

But maybe they could fight off the notion of their own helplessness, as Sayid had. He didn't have enough money to go to college like his older brothers, and after three years with the National Youth Corps, assigned to development projects around the country, he had spent his last two holidays knocking on the doors of businesses in Nairobi without success. Still, he seemed certain that persistence would pay off.

"To get a job these days, even as a clerk, requires that you know somebody," Sayid said as we approached Granny's compound. "Or bribe someone. That's why I would like to start my own business. That was your father's error, I think. For all his brilliance, he never had something of his own."

He thought for a moment. "Of course, there's no point wasting time worrying about the mistakes of the past. Like this dispute over your father's inheritance. From the beginning, I have told my sisters to forget this thing. We must get on with our lives. They do not listen to me, though. And in the meantime, the money they fight over goes where? To the lawyers. How does the saying go? When two locusts fight, it is always the crow who feasts."

THE NEXT DAY Roy told me that he was hitching a ride to Kendu Bay with the principal of a nearby school. He said that I should come, too, and pay my respects to the family there. Sayid and I went to gather a change of clothes and piled into the principal's old jalopy along with Kezia, Roy, and Bernard.

It was a very long journey, and by the time we got there it

was nearly evening. After dinner, we set off down a narrow footpath, under a full moon, and arrived at a small house where the shadows of moths fluttered against a yellow window. In a small back room, in front of a kerosene lamp, I was introduced to what looked like the oldest man I had ever seen. His hair was snow-white, his skin like parchment. He was motionless, his eyes closed. I thought perhaps he was asleep, but then the old man's head tilted in my direction, and I saw a mirror image of the face I'd seen the day before in a faded photograph on Granny's wall.

Roy explained who I was, and the old man nodded and began to speak in a low, quaking voice.

"He says that he is glad you have come," Roy translated. "He was your grandfather's brother. He wishes you well."

I said that I was happy to see him, and the old man nodded again.

"He says that many young men have been lost to . . . the white man's country. He says his own son is in America and has not come home for many years. Such men are like ghosts, he says. When they die, no one will be there to mourn them. No ancestors will be there to welcome them. So . . . he says it is good that you have returned."

The old man raised his hand and I shook it gently. As we got up to leave, he said something else, and Roy nodded before closing the door behind us.

"He says that if you hear of his son," Roy explained, "you should tell him to come home."

Later that evening, Sayid told me that my father had been very popular in these parts. "Whenever he came home, he would buy everyone drinks and stay out very late. The people would tell him, 'You are a big man, but you have not forgotten us.' Such words made him happy, I think. I remember once, he took me to Kisumu town in his Mercedes. On the way, he saw a *matatu* picking up passengers, and he said to me, 'Sayid, we will be *matatu* drivers this evening!' At the next *matatu* stop, he picked up the remaining people and told me to collect the regular fare from them. I think we squeezed eight people into his car. He took them wherever they needed to go. And when each of them got out, he gave them all their money back. After we were done, we went to the bar, and he told the story to all of his friends. He laughed very well that night."

Sayid paused, choosing his words carefully.

"This is what made my brother such a good man. But I think also that once you are one thing, you cannot pretend that you are something else. How could he be a *matatu* driver, or stay out all night drinking, and also succeed in writing Kenya's economic plan? Even though he prided himself on his independence, I think my brother was afraid that if he changed too much he would no longer belong with those he'd grown up with."

"I don't want to be that way," Bernard said.

Sayid looked at his nephew with something like regret. "I did not mean to speak so freely, Bernard. You must respect your elders. They clear the way for you so that your path is easier. But if you see them falling into a pit, then you must learn to what?"

"Step around," Bernard said.

"You are right. Depart from that path and make your own."

CHAPTER 18

The next day I made the trip back to Home Squared with Sayid and Bernard. We found the women gathered on straw mats under the shade of a mango tree, Granny braiding Auma's hair, Zeituni braiding the hair of a neighbor girl. I sat down beside them and asked Granny, with Auma translating, to start at the beginning. How did our great-grandfather Obama come to live in Kendu? Where did our grandfather work? Why did the Old Man's mother leave?

And under the shade of a mango tree, our voices ran together, three generations tumbling over each other like the currents of a slow-moving stream . . .

First there was Miwiru. It's not known who came before. Miwiru sired Sigoma, Sigoma sired Owiny, Owiny sired Kisodhi, Kisodhi sired Ogelo, Ogelo sired Otondi, Otondi sired Obongo, Obongo sired

Okoth, and Okoth sired Opiyo. The women who bore them, their names are forgotten, for that was the way of our people.

Okoth lived in Alego. Before that, it is known only that families traveled a great distance, from the direction of what is now Uganda, and that we were like the Masai, migrating in search of water and grazing land for great herds of cattle. In Alego, the people settled and began to grow crops.

As the land in Alego became crowded, Opiyo decided to move to Kendu Bay. He had no land, but it was the custom of our people that a man could use any that was not taken. He worked in the compounds of other men and cleared the land for his own farm. But he died very young, leaving behind two wives and several children. One wife was taken in by Opiyo's brother, as was the custom then—she became the brother's wife, her children his children. But the other wife also died, and her oldest son, Obama, was orphaned when still a boy. He, too, lived with his uncle, but the family was poor, and Obama began to work for other men as his father had done before him.

The family he worked for was wealthy, but they came to admire Obama, for he was enterprising and a very good farmer. When he sought to marry their oldest daughter, they agreed. And when this daughter died, they agreed that Obama could marry the younger daughter, whose name was Nyaoke. Eventually Obama had four wives, who bore him many children. He became prosperous, with a large compound and many cattle and goats. And because of his responsible ways, he became an elder in Kendu, and many came to seek his advice.

Your grandfather, Onyango, was the fifth son of Obama and Nyaoke.

Even as a boy, Onyango was strange. He would wander off on his own for many days, and when he returned he would not say where he had been. He was very serious always—he never laughed or played games with the other children, and never made jokes. He was always curious about other people's business, which is how he came to sit in the hut of an herbalist, a man who turned plants into medicine, and to learn his art.

When your grandfather was still a boy, we began to hear that the white man had come to nearby Kisumu town. It was said that these white men had skin as soft as a child's, but that they rode on a ship that roared like thunder and had sticks that burst with fire. Before this, no one in our village had seen white men—only Arab traders who came to sell us sugar and cloth. But even that was rare, for our people did not use much sugar, and we did not wear cloth, only a goatskin that covered our genitals. So the elders advised the men to stay away from Kisumu until this white man was better understood.

Despite this warning, Onyango became curious and decided that he must see these white men for himself. One day he disappeared, and no one knew where he had gone. Then, many months later, while his brothers were working the land, Onyango returned to the village. He was wearing the trousers of a white man, and a shirt like a white man, and shoes that covered his feet. The small children were frightened, and his brothers didn't know what to make of this change.

"What has happened to you?" his father, Obama, asked. "Why do you wear these strange skins?" Onyango said nothing, and Obama decided that Onyango must be wearing trousers to hide the fact that he was circumcised, which was against Luo custom. He thought that Onyango's shirt must be covering a rash, or sores. Obama turned to his other sons and said, "Don't go near this brother of yours. He is unclean." Then he returned to his hut, and the others laughed and shunned Onyango. Because of this, Onyango returned to Kisumu, and would remain separated from his father for the rest of his life.

Nobody realized that the white man intended to stay. We thought they had only come to trade their goods. Some built a religious mission and spoke of their god, who they said was all-powerful. But most people thought their talk was silly. Even when white men appeared with rifles, we didn't resist because we hadn't seen how deadly they were. Many thought the guns were fancy stirrers for *ugali*, the cornmeal porridge we ate.

Things began to change with the first of the white man's wars. A district commissioner arrived—we called him *Bwana Ogalo*, "the Oppressor"—and he told us we had to pay a tax on our huts with the white man's money. Many men began to fight and were beaten or shot and their huts burned to the ground.

Onyango had learned to read and write English, which made him useful to the white man. During the war he was put in charge of road crews. When he finally returned, he cleared land for himself in Kendu but away from his father's compound, and he rarely spoke to his brothers. He chose to live in a tent instead of a hut. People had never seen such a thing and they thought he was crazy. After he had staked his claim, he traveled to Nairobi, where a white man had offered him a job.

He was not the only one who moved to town. After the war, many Africans began working for the white man's money. The war had brought famine and disease as well as large numbers of white settlers, who were allowed to seize the best land. Respect for tradition weakened. Beer now came in bottles, and many men became drunks. More fathers agreed to send their children to the mission schools, but even the children who got an education were not allowed to do the things the white man did. Only white people were allowed to buy certain land and run certain businesses. Many of us began to taste the white man's life, and we decided that compared to him, our lives were poor.

By these standards, your grandfather prospered. He thought many things the white man did were foolish or unjust and would not allow himself to be beaten. Once he was arrested for thrashing his white employer, who had tried to cane him. He used the man's own cane! But he respected the white man's power. He would say that the white man was always improving himself, whereas the African was suspicious of anything new. So he learned how to prepare the white man's food and organize the white man's house. Because of this, he worked in the estates of some of the most important white men. He saved his wages and bought land and cattle in Kendu.

Finally, he found a wife, Helima. No one knows how she felt toward your grandfather, but she was quiet and polite—and most important, she could maintain his high housekeeping standards. He built a hut for her in Kendu, where she spent most of her time. After a few years, it was discovered that Helima could not have any children. Among the Luo, this was grounds for divorce. But your grandfather chose to keep Helima, and in that sense, he treated her well.

Still, it must have been lonely for Helima, for your grandfather worked all the time and had no time for friends or entertainment. He did not drink with other men, and he did not smoke. His only pleasure was going to the dance halls in Nairobi once a month. But he also was not such a good dancer—he was rough, and would bump into people and step on their feet. Most people did not say anything because they knew Onyango had a temper. One night, though, a drunken man complained about Onyango's clumsiness and then mocked him for being unable to have children.

People who overheard the conversation began to laugh, and Onyango beat this man severely. But the drunk man's words must have stayed with your grandfather, for that month he set out to find another wife. Finally he chose a young and beautiful girl named Akumu. Even though she was pledged to another man, he bribed her father with cattle. The next day, your grandfather's friends captured Akumu while she was walking in the forest and dragged her back to Onyango's hut.

The young boy, Godfrey, appeared with a washbasin, and we all washed our hands for lunch. Auma stood up to stretch her back, her hair still half undone, a troubled look on her face. She said something to Granny, and drew a long response.

"I was asking her about grabbing the woman, which was part of Luo custom," said Auma. "Traditionally, once the man pays the dowry, the woman must not seem too eager to be with him. She pretends to refuse him, and so the man's friends must capture her and take her back to his hut. Only after this ritual do they perform a proper marriage ceremony."

Auma took a small bite of her food. "I told her that some women might not have been pretending."

Zeituni dipped her *ugali* into the stew. "Yah, Auma, it was not as bad as you say. If her husband behaved badly, the girl could always leave."

"But what good was that if her father would only end up choosing someone else for her? Tell me, what would happen if a woman refused her father's choice of a suitor?"

Zeituni shrugged. "She shamed herself and her family."

"You see?" Auma turned to ask Granny something, and whatever Granny said in response made Auma hit her—only half playfully—on the arm.

"I asked her if the man would force the girl to sleep with him the night of her capture," Auma explained, "and she told me that no one knew what went on in a man's hut. But she also asked me how a man would know if he wanted the whole bowl of soup unless he first had a taste."

I asked Granny how old she had been when she married

our grandfather. Granny told us she had been just sixteen when she married; our grandfather was a friend of her father's. I asked if that bothered her, and she shook her head.

"She says it was common to marry an older man," Auma said. "She says in those days, marriage involved more than just two people. It brought together families and affected the whole village. You didn't complain, or worry about love. If you didn't learn to love your husband, you learned to obey him."

At this point, Auma and Granny began to speak at length, and Granny said something that again made the others laugh. Everyone except Auma, who stood up and began to stack the dishes.

"I give up," Auma said, exasperated.

"What did Granny say?"

"I asked her why our women put up with the arranged marriage. The way men make all the decisions. The wife-beating. She said that often the women needed to be beaten, because otherwise they would not do everything that was required of them. You see how we are? We complain, but still we encourage men to treat us with no respect."

Granny's voice suddenly became serious.

"Perhaps if I were young today," she said in Luo, "I would not have accepted these things. Perhaps I would only care about my feelings, and falling in love. But that's not the world I was raised in. I only know what I have seen. What I have not seen does not make my heart heavy."

After we finished eating, Auma and the neighbor's girl

resumed their positions in front of the older women, and Granny returned to her story.

By the time I came to live with Onyango, Akumu had given birth to two children. The first was Sarah. Three years later came Barack, your father. I did not know Akumu well, but I could see that she was unhappy. Her spirit was rebellious, and she found Onyango too demanding. Perhaps she still loved the man she was supposed to marry before Onyango took her away. More than once, Akumu ran away, but Onyango would follow her and bring her back.

Life became easier for her when the Second World War came. Your grandfather went overseas as the cook to the British captain, and I came to live with Akumu and Helima, helping both with the children and their crops. Onyango traveled widely with the British regiments, and we did not see him for some time. When he returned three years later, he came with a gramophone and a picture of another woman he claimed to have married in Burma.

Onyango was now almost fifty. More and more, he thought of quitting his work for the white man and returning to farm the land. He saw, though, that the land surrounding Kendu was crowded and overgrazed. So he decided to go back to Alego, the land that his grandfather had abandoned.

When we arrived in Alego, most of this land that you now see was bush, and life was hard for all of us. But your grandfather had studied modern farming techniques while in Nairobi, and he could make anything grow. In less than a year he had enough crops to sell at market. He planted the mango and banana and pawpaw trees that you see today.

He built large huts for Akumu and myself and a hut of his own. He had brought back a crystal set from England that he displayed on a shelf, and on his gramophone he played strange music late into the night. When my first children, Omar and Zeituni, were born, he bought them cribs and gowns and mosquito nets, just as he had for Barack and Sarah. In the cooking hut, he built an oven in which he baked bread and cakes like you buy in a store.

His neighbors in Alego had never seen such things. At first they were suspicious of him and thought he was foolish. But soon they came to respect his generosity, as well as what he taught them about farming and herbal medicines.

Akumu was perpetually unhappy. Onyango beat her, and she often argued with him. She was also proud and scornful of me, and often refused to help in the household chores. She had a third child—named Auma, like this one sitting here—and as she nursed this new baby, she secretly planned her escape.

One night, when Sarah was twelve and Barack was nine, Akumu woke up Sarah and said that she was running away to Kendu. She told Sarah that it was too difficult a journey for children to make at night but that they should follow her as soon as they were older. Then she disappeared with her baby into the darkness.

When Onyango found out what had happened, he was furious. At first he thought he should let Akumu go, but when he saw that Barack and Sarah were still young, and that even I, with two children of my own, was little more than a girl, he went to Akumu's family in Kendu and asked that she be returned. But the family refused. They had heard how harshly Onyango treated Akumu, and, in fact, had already accepted the dowry for Akumu's remarriage to another man. Together Akumu and her new husband had already left for Tanganyika. There was nothing Onyango could do, so he told me that I was now the mother of all his children.

But Sarah remembered her mother's instructions, and only a few weeks passed before she woke up Barack in the middle of the night, just as her mother had done to her. She told Barack to be quiet, helped him get dressed, and together they walked down the road to Kendu. I still wonder that they survived. They were gone for almost two weeks, walking many miles each day, hiding from those who passed them on the road, sleeping in fields and begging for food. Not far from Kendu, they became lost, and a woman saw them and took pity on them, for they were filthy and almost starved. When she realized who they were she sent for your grandfather. And when Onyango came to get them, and saw how badly they looked, this is the only time that anyone ever saw him cry.

The children never tried to run away again. But I don't think they ever forgot their journey. Sarah kept a careful distance from Onyango, and in her heart remained loyal to Akumu, for she was older, and perhaps had seen how the old man had treated her mother. I believe she also resented me for taking her mother's place. Barack reacted differently. He could not forgive his mother for having abandoned him and acted as if Akumu didn't exist. He told everyone that I was his mother, and although he sent Akumu money when he became a man, to the end of his life he always acted coldly toward her.

The strange thing was that in many ways Sarah was more like her father—strict, hardworking, easy to anger. Whereas Barack was wild and stubborn like Akumu.

As you might expect, Onyango was very strict with his children. He worked them hard, and would not allow them to play outside the compound, because he said other children were filthy and ill-mannered. Whenever Onyango went away, I would ignore these instructions, because children must play with other children, just as they must eat and sleep. But I would never tell your grandfather what I did, and I would have to scrub the children clean before your grandfather came home.

This was not easy, especially with Barack. That boy was so mischievous! In Onyango's presence, he appeared well-mannered and obedient. But behind the old man's back, Barack did as he pleased. When Onyango was away on business, Barack would take off his proper clothes and go off with other boys to wrestle or swim in the river, to steal the fruit from the neighbors' trees or ride their cows. I would always cover up his foolishness, for I loved him as my own son.

Although he did not like to show it, your grandfather was very fond of Barack, because the boy was so clever. When Barack was only a baby, Onyango would teach him the alphabet and numbers, and it was not long before the son could outdo the father in these things. This pleased Onyango, for to him knowledge was the source of all the white man's power, and he wanted to make sure that his son was as educated as any white man. He was less concerned with Sarah's education, although she was quick like Barack. Most men thought educating their daughters was a waste of money.

This created more friction between Sarah and her younger brother, especially because she knew that Barack was not always serious about his studies.

Everything came too easily to him. At first he went to the mission school nearby, but he came back after the first day and told his father that he could not study there because his class was taught by a woman and he knew everything she had to teach him. The next closest school was six miles away, and I began to walk him to this school every morning.

His teacher there was a man, but Barack discovered that this didn't solve his problems. He always knew the answers, and sometimes would even correct the teacher's mistakes before the whole class. This caused Barack many canings at the hand of the headmaster. But it also might have taught him something, because the next year, when he switched to a class with a woman teacher, I noticed that he didn't complain.

Still, he was bored with school, and when he became older, he would stop going for weeks at a time. A few days before exams, he would find a classmate and read through the lessons. He could sit down and teach himself everything in just a few days, and when the marks came in, he would always be first. The few times he was not, he came to me in tears, for he was so used to being the best. But usually he would come home laughing and boasting of his cleverness.

By the time your father was a teenager, things were changing rapidly in Kenya. People began to talk about independence. There were meetings and demonstrations, and petitions were presented to the government, complaining about white people taking land. Like other boys, your father was influenced by the early talk of independence. But your grandfather doubted that the movement would lead to anything, because he thought Africans could never win against the white man's army.

Despite his attitude, your grandfather was once held in a detention camp for six months. Another African, a tax collector, was jealous of his lands and had once been scolded by your grandfather for pocketing some of the tax money. This man told the authorities that Onyango was a rebel, and one day soldiers came to take your grandfather away. Eventually he was found innocent, but he was in the camp for over six months, and when he returned to Alego he was very thin and dirty. He had difficulty walking, and his head was full of lice. He was so ashamed, he refused to enter his house or tell us what had happened.

Barack was away at the time and only learned about this detention later. He had taken the district examination, and had been admitted to Maseno Mission School, some fifty miles south. This should have been a great honor for Barack, since only the best students got into Maseno. But your father's rebellious nature caused the school much grief. He would sneak girls into his dormitory. He and his friends would raid farms for chickens and yams because they did not like the dormitory food. The teachers overlooked much of this, for they saw how smart he was. But eventually Barack went too far and was expelled.

Onyango was so furious when he found out that he beat Barack with a stick until Barack's back was bleeding. But Barack refused to run or cry out, or even explain himself to his father.

Barack moved to Nairobi and found a job working as a clerk for the railway. But he was bored, and he became distracted by the Kenyan independence movement. He began to attend meetings and came to know some of the rebel leaders. At one of these meetings, the police burst in, and Barack was jailed. He sent word to his father that he needed money for bail, but Onyango refused. He told me that he needed to teach his son a lesson.

Because he was not a leader, Barack was released after a few days. But he had begun to think that what his father had once told him was true—that he would amount to nothing. He was a man of twenty and had no money or prospects. And he now had a wife and a child. He had met Kezia when he was only eighteen. One year after they married, Roy was born. Two years later came your sister, Auma.

Barack was deeply depressed, almost desperate. He saw that he might end up working as a clerk for the rest of his life. Then, good fortune struck. He met two American women who were teaching at a religious organization. When they saw how smart he was, they arranged for him to take a correspondence course that would give him the certificate he needed to go to college. If he was successful, they said, they would try to help him get into a university in America.

Barack became very excited and for the first time in his life, he worked diligently. Every night, and during his lunch hours, he would study. A few months later, he took the exam at the American embassy. The exam took several months to grade, and during this wait he was so nervous he could barely eat. He became so thin that we thought he would die. One day, the letter came. I was not there to see him open it. I know that when he told me the news, he was still shouting out with happiness.

He had no money, though, and no university had yet accepted him. Onyango had softened toward his son when he saw that he was becoming more responsible, but even he could not raise enough money. So Barack wrote to universities in America. He wrote and he wrote. Finally, a university in Hawaii wrote back and told him they would give him a scholarship. No one knew where this place was, but Barack didn't care. He dropped off his pregnant wife and son with me, and in less than a month he was gone.

What happened in America, I cannot say. I know

that after less than two years we received a letter saying that he had met this American girl, Ann, your mother, and that he would like to marry her.

Now, Barry, I know you have heard that your grandfather disapproved of this marriage. This is true, but it is not for the reasons you say. Onyango did not believe your father was behaving responsibly. He wrote to Barack, saying, "How can you marry this white woman when you have responsibilities at home? Will this woman return with you and live as a Luo woman? Will she accept that you already have a wife and children? I have not heard of white people understanding such things. Their women are jealous and used to being pampered. But if I am wrong in this matter, let the girl's father come to my hut and discuss the situation properly. For these are the affairs of elders, not children." He also wrote to your grandfather Stanley and said many of these same things.

As you know, your father went ahead with the marriage. He told Onyango what had happened only after you were born. We are all happy that this marriage took place, because without it we would not have you here with us now. But your grandfather was very angry and threatened to have Barack's visa revoked. And because he had lived with white people, perhaps Onyango did understand the white people's customs better than Barack did. For when Barack returned to

Kenya, we discovered that you and your mother had stayed behind, just as Onyango had warned.

Soon after Barack came, a white woman arrived in Kisumu looking for him. At first we thought this must be your mother, Ann. Barack had to explain that this was a different woman, Ruth. He said that he had met her at Harvard and that she had followed him to Kenya without his knowledge.

Once Barack married Ruth, she could not accept the idea of his having Kezia as a second wife. So Kezia was left behind and Auma and Roy went to live in Nairobi with Barack and Ruth. When your father brought Auma and Roy back to visit us, Ruth would refuse to accompany him and would not let Barack bring their children, David and Mark.

The others have told you what happened to your father in Nairobi. We saw him rarely, and he would usually stay only a short time. Whenever he came, he would bring us expensive gifts and money and impress all the people with his big car and fine clothes. But your grandfather continued to speak harshly to him, as if he were a boy. Onyango was now very old. He walked with a cane and was almost blind. He could not even bathe without my help, which I think caused him shame. But age did not soften his temper.

Later, when Barack fell from power, he would try to hide his problems from your grandfather.

Only to me would he confide his unhappiness and disappointments. I would tell him he was too stubborn in his dealings with the government. He would talk to me about principles, and I would tell him that his principles weighed heavily on his children. He would say I didn't understand, just as his father had said to me. So I stopped giving advice and just listened.

That is what Barack needed most, I think—someone to listen to him. Even after things had improved and he had built this house for us, he remained heavy-hearted. With his children, he behaved just as Onyango had behaved toward him. He saw that he was pushing them away, but there was nothing he could do. He still liked to boast and laugh and drink with the men. But his laughter was empty.

I remember the last time he visited Onyango before the old man died. The two of them sat in their chairs, facing each other and eating their food, but no words passed between them. A few months later, when Onyango finally went to join his ancestors, Barack came home to make all the arrangements. He said very little, and it is only when he sorted through a few of the old man's belongings that I saw him weep.

Granny stood up and brushed the grass off her skirt. "It's going to rain," she said, and we all gathered up the mats and cups and carried them into the house.

Inside, I asked Granny if she had anything left of the Old Man's or our grandfather's. She pulled out an old leather trunk and gave me a rust-colored book the size of a passport, along with a few papers of different colors, stapled together and chewed along one side.

"I'm afraid this is all I could find," she said to Auma. "The rats got to the papers before I had a chance to put them away."

The binding on the red book had crumbled, but the cover was still legible: *Domestic Servant's Pocket Register*, it read, and in smaller letters, *Issued under the Authority of the Registration of Domestic Servant's Ordinance, 1928, Colony and Protectorate of Kenya*. On the inside cover, we found a two-shilling stamp above Onyango's left and right thumbprints. The swirls of his thumbs were still clear, but the box where the photograph had been was empty.

The book gave a definition of the word *servant: cook, house servant, waiter, butler, nurse, valet, bar boy, footmen, or chauffeur, or washerman*. It said that any servant found working without a passbook, or damaging a passbook, would have to pay a fine of up to one hundred shillings, be imprisoned for up to six months, or both.

Most important, there were the personal details of this Registered Servant, my grandfather:

Name: *Hussein II Onyango.*
Native Registration Ordinance No.: *Rwl A NBI 0976717.*
Race or Tribe: *Ja'Luo.*

Usual Place of Residence When Not Employed: *Kisumu.*

Sex: *M.*

Age: *35.*

Height and Build: *6'0" Medium.*

Complexion: *Dark.*

Nose: *Flat.*

Mouth: *Large.*

Hair: *Curly.*

Teeth: *Six Missing.*

Scars, Tribal Marks, or Other Peculiarities: *None.*

Toward the back of the book, we found testimonials from his employers. Capt. C. Harford of Nairobi's Government House said that Onyango *"performed his duties as personal boy with admirable diligence."* Mr. A. G. Dickson found his cooking excellent—*"he can read and write English and follows any recipes . . . apart from other things his pastries are excellent."* On the other hand, Mr. Arthur W. H. Cole of the East Africa Survey Group said that after a week on the job, Onyango was *"found to be unsuitable and certainly not worth 60 shillings per month."*

We moved to the stack of letters. There were more than thirty of them, from our father to the presidents of various universities in the United States.

Dear President Calhoun, one letter began. *I have heard of your college from Mrs. Helen Roberts of Palo Alto, California, who is now in Nairobi here. Mrs. Roberts, knowing how much desirous I am to further my studies in the United States of America, has asked me to apply to your esteemed college for admission. I shall therefore be very much pleased if you will kindly forward me your application form and information regarding the possibility of such scholarships as you may be aware of.*

This was it, I thought. My inheritance.

I rearranged the letters in a neat stack and set them under the registry book. Then I went out to the backyard and stood before the two graves. Everything around me—the cornfields, the mango tree, the sky—seemed to be closing in, until I was left with only a series of images, Granny's stories come to life.

I see my grandfather, Onyango, standing before his father's hut in his white man's clothing. I watch his father turn away and hear his brothers laugh, and feel—as he must have felt—the sudden jump in his heart. As he turns and starts back down the red earth road, I know that the path of his life has permanently changed.

He will have to reinvent himself in this dry, solitary place. Through force of will, he will create a life out of the scraps of an unknown world, and the memories of a world that has become obsolete. I see him as an old man sitting alone in a freshly scrubbed hut and know that he still hears his father and brothers laughing at him. He still feels the humiliation of being a servant—of standing silently as a British captain explains for the third and last time the correct way to mix a gin and tonic. The nerves in my grandfather's neck tighten, the rage builds—he grabs his stick to hit at something, anything. Until finally his grip weakens. He realizes that no matter how strong he is, he cannot outrun the laughter and humiliations. His body goes limp. He waits to die, alone.

The picture fades, replaced by the image of a nine-year-old boy—my father. He's hungry, tired, clinging to his sister's hand, searching for the mother he has lost. Finally, it is too much for him, and the slender cord that holds him to his mother snaps, sending her image to float down, down into the emptiness. The boy starts to cry; he shakes off his sister's hand. He wants to go home, he shouts, back to his father's house. He will find a new mother. He will learn the power of his own mind.

But he won't forget the desperation of that day. Twelve years later, at his narrow desk in a job with no future, he will feel that same panic return. He, too, will have to reinvent himself. He pulls out a list of addresses, yanks the typewriter toward him, and begins to type, letter after letter after letter, sealing them up like messages in bottles.

How lucky he must have felt when that letter of acceptance came from Hawaii. He had been chosen after all; he possessed the grace of his name, the *baraka*, the blessings of God. With a college degree, the right wardrobe, the American wife, the car, the words, the wallet, the proper proportion of tonic to gin, what could stand in his way?

He had almost succeeded, in a way his own father could never have hoped for. And then, after seeming to travel so far, he discovered that he had not escaped after all! He was still trapped on his father's island, and his mother was still gone, gone, away. . . .

I dropped to the ground and swept my hand across the smooth yellow tile.

Oh, Father, I cried. There was no shame in your confusion. Just as there was no shame in your father's before you. If only you both had not been silent.

It was the silence that betrayed us.

If it weren't for that silence, your grandfather might have told your father that even if he escaped his village and dressed like a white man and learned the white man's ways, he could never escape who he was or where he had come from. He could never create a new identity alone, by turning away completely from the world that had shaped him.

Your father might have taught those same lessons to you.

And you, the son, might have taught something to your father. You might have shown him that the new world he embraced, the world of railroads and indoor toilets and gramophones, had a dangerous power. Because of that power, your father—my grandfather—lost a faith born out of hardship, a faith that wasn't new, that wasn't Black or white or Christian or Muslim, but that pulsed in the heart of the first Kenyan village and the first Kansas homestead—a faith in other people.

The silence killed your faith. And without it you clung to too much of your past. And too little. Too much of its rigidness, its suspicions, its male cruelties. Too little of the laughter in Granny's voice, the pleasures of company while herding the goats, the murmur of the market, the stories around the fire.

For all your gifts—your quick mind, your charm—you could never be whole if you left that precious legacy behind.

For a long time I sat between the two graves and wept. When I had no more tears left to cry, I felt a calmness wash over me. I felt the circle finally close. I saw that my life in America—the Black life, the white life, the sense of abandonment I'd felt as a boy, the frustration and hope I'd witnessed in Chicago—all of it was connected to this small plot of earth an ocean away, connected by more than the accident of a name or the color of my skin. The pain I felt was my father's pain. My questions were my brothers' questions. Their struggle was my struggle.

A light rain began to fall, and I felt a hand on my arm. I turned to find Bernard beside me, trying to fit the two of us under a bent-up old umbrella.

"They wanted me to see if you were okay," he said.

I smiled. "Yeah. I'm okay. Let's take a walk."

We stood up and started toward the entrance to the compound. The young boy, Godfrey, was leaning against the mud wall of the cooking hut. He looked at us and smiled shyly.

"Come on," Bernard said, waving to the boy. "You can walk with us." And so the three of us made our way over the widening dirt road, picking at leaves that grew along the way, watching the rain blow down across the valleys.

EPILOGUE

I remained in Kenya for two more weeks. We all went back to Nairobi and there were more dinners, more arguments, more stories. Granny stayed in Auma's apartment, and each night I fell asleep to their whispering voices. One day we gathered at a photography studio for a family portrait, and all the women wore flowing African gowns of bright greens and yellows and blues, and the men were all tall and clean-shaven and neatly pressed, and the photographer told us what a handsome picture we made.

Roy flew back to Washington, D.C., soon after that, and Granny returned to Home Squared. The days suddenly became very quiet, and a certain sadness settled over Auma and me, as if we were coming out of a dream.

On the last weekend of my stay, Auma and I took the train to the coast and stayed at an old beachfront hotel in Mombasa that had once been a favorite of the Old Man's. We didn't do much, just read and swam and walked along the beach, watching pale crabs scurry like ghosts into their sandy holes. We visited Mombasa's Old Town and climbed the worn stairs of a fort built by the Portuguese, now an empty casing of stone, its massive walls peeling like papier-mâché, its empty cannons pointing out to a tranquil sea.

On the way back to Nairobi, Auma and I decided to splurge, buying tickets on a bus line that actually assigned seats. But my knees ended up being pinched by a passenger who wanted his money's worth from the reclining seats, and a sudden rainstorm sent water streaming through leaks in the roof, which we tried—unsuccessfully—to plug with tissue.

Eventually, the rain stopped, and we found ourselves looking out at a barren landscape of gravel and shrub and the occasional baobab tree. I remembered reading somewhere that the baobab could go for years without flowering, surviving on barely any rainfall; and seeing the trees there in the hazy afternoon light, I understood why people believed they had a special power—that they housed ancestral spirits and demons, that humankind first appeared under such a tree.

"They look as if each one could tell a story," Auma said, and it was true. Each tree seemed to possess its own character—not generous, not cruel, but simply enduring, with secrets whose depths I would never plumb. They looked as if they might uproot themselves and simply walk away, if it weren't for the knowledge that on this earth one place is not so different from another—the knowledge that one moment carries within it all that's gone on before.

AS I WRITE, it has been six years since that first trip to Kenya, and much in the world has changed.

For me, it has been a relatively quiet period, a time of doing the things we tell ourselves we finally must do to grow up. I went to Harvard Law School, spending most of three years in libraries. The study of law can be disappointing at times, a matter of applying narrow rules to a reality that sometimes won't cooperate. Often the law helps those who are already powerful manage that power—and seeks to explain to everyone else why it is fair that they should remain powerless.

But that's not all the law is. The law is also a means for a nation to examine its conscience and ask the very same questions that have come to shape my life, the same questions that I sometimes, late at night, find myself asking the Old Man—about the definition of *community* and the ways we are all responsible to one another. The answers I find in law books don't always satisfy me. And yet I believe that so long as the questions are still being asked, there is hope that what binds us together will prove stronger than what drives us apart.

I think I've learned to be more patient these past few years, with others as well as myself. If so, I give most of the credit to my wife, Michelle. She's a daughter of Chicago's South Side, raised in one of those bungalow-style houses that I spent so many hours visiting during my first year in Chicago. She doesn't always know what to think of me; she worries that, like Gramps and the Old Man, I am something of a dreamer. Sometimes, with her practicality and Midwestern attitudes, she reminds me a lot of Toot. In fact, the first time I took her back to Hawaii, Toot described my bride-to-be as "a very sensible girl"—which Michelle understood to be my grandmother's highest form of praise.

After our engagement, I took Michelle to Africa to meet the other half of my family. She was an immediate success there as well, partly because she soon had a much bigger Luo vocabulary than I did. We had a fine time in Alego, helping Auma on a film project, listening to more of Granny's stories, meeting relatives I'd missed the first time around. Away from the countryside, though, life in Kenya seemed to have gotten harder. The economy had gotten worse, the government seemed more corrupt, and street crime was on the rise. The case of the Old Man's inheritance was still up in the air, and Sarah and Kezia were still not speaking to each other. Neither Bernard, nor Abo, nor Sayid had found steady work, although they remained hopeful.

Michelle's father, as good and decent a man as I've ever known, died before we were married. Gramps died of prostate cancer a few months later. As a World War II veteran, he was buried at Punchbowl National Cemetery on a hill overlooking Honolulu. It was a small ceremony with a few of his bridge and golf partners in attendance, a three-gun salute, and a bugle playing taps.

Despite these heartaches, Michelle and I decided to go ahead with our wedding plans. The service took place in the sanctuary of Trinity United Church of Christ. Everyone looked very fine at the reception, my new aunts admiring the cake, my new uncles admiring themselves in their rented tuxedos. My organizing friend Johnnie was there, sharing a laugh with some of my old friends from Hawaii. So were Angela, Shirley, and Mona, who told my mother what a fine job she'd done raising me. ("You don't know the half of it," my mother replied with a laugh.)

I looked at my baby sister, Maya, and saw a full-grown woman, beautiful and wise and looking like a Latin countess with her olive skin and long black hair and black bridesmaid's gown. Auma was standing beside her, looking just as lovely, although her eyes were a little puffy—to my surprise she was the only one who cried during the ceremony.

When the band started to play, the two of them sought out Michelle's five- and six-year-old cousins, who had been our ring-bearers. Watching the boys lead my sisters out onto the dance floor, I thought they looked like young African princes in their little kente-cloth caps and matching cummerbunds and wilted bow ties.

The person who made me proudest of all, though, was Roy. Actually, now we call him Abongo, his Luo name, for two years ago he decided to embrace his African heritage.

He converted to Islam, and no longer drank or smoked. He still worked at his accounting firm, but talked about moving back to Kenya once he had enough money. In fact, when we saw each other last in Home Squared, he was busy building a hut for himself and his mother, away from our grandfather's compound. He told me that he had moved forward with his import business and hoped it would soon pay enough to employ Bernard and Abo full-time. And when we went together to stand by the Old Man's grave, I noticed there was finally a plaque where the bare cement had been.

Abongo's new lifestyle has left him lean and clear-eyed, and at the wedding, he looked so dignified in his black African gown with white trim and matching cap that some of our guests thought he might be my father. He was certainly an older brother that day, talking me through my nerves, patiently telling me for the fifth and sixth time that yes, he still had the wedding ring, and that if I spent any more time in front of the mirror it wouldn't matter how I looked because we were sure to be late.

Toward the end of the wedding, I watched him grinning widely for the video camera, his long arms draped over the shoulders of my mother and Toot, whose heads barely reached the height of his chest. "Eh, brother," he said to me as I walked up to the three of them. "It looks like I have two new mothers now." Toot patted him on the back. "And we have a new son," she said, although when she tried to say "Abongo" her Kansas tongue mangled it hopelessly. My mother's chin started to tremble like it does when she's about to cry, and Abongo lifted up his glass of fruit punch for a toast.

"To those who are not here with us," he said.

"And to a happy ending," I said.

We dribbled our drinks onto the checkered-tile floor. And for that moment, at least, I felt like the luckiest man alive.

POSTSCRIPT

July 2004

Most of the characters in this book—some of whose names have been changed to protect their privacy—are still a part of my life.

The exception is my mother, who died of cancer in 1995, a few months after *Dreams from My Father* was first published. She handled her illness with grace and good humor, and she helped my sister Maya and me push on with our lives, in spite of how much we dreaded losing her.

She had spent the ten years before that doing what she loved. She traveled the world, working in distant villages of Africa and Asia, helping women buy a sewing machine or a milk cow or an education. She gathered friends from high and low, took long walks, and stared at the moon. She wrote reports, read novels, pestered her children, and dreamed of grandchildren.

We saw each other often, our bond unbroken. As I wrote this book, she read the drafts, correcting stories that I had misunderstood. She was careful not to comment on the passages about her but quick to defend my father if she felt I was being too harsh.

Sometimes I think that if I had known she would not live much longer, I might have written a different book—less a meditation on my absent parent, and more a celebration of the one who was the single constant in my life. In my daughters I see her every day, her joy, her capacity for wonder. I won't try to describe how deeply I still mourn her passing. I know that she was the kindest, most generous spirit I have ever known, and that what is best in me I owe to her.

PHOTOGRAPH CREDITS

ACKNOWLEDGMENTS

I am grateful to Rachel Klayman, my longtime editor at Crown, for taking the original, much lengthier version of this book and deftly adapting it for younger readers.

At Crown, I'd also like to thank David Drake, who ably orchestrated the publication of this edition, and Chris Brand, who reenvisioned the book's cover for a new audience. Madison Jacobs and Lydia Morgan energetically tracked every detail and kept the project moving forward. Special thanks to Barbara Bachman at Random House and to freelancer Renee Harleston.

As always, I am lucky to have the hard work and steady support of my staff, notably Anita Decker Breckenridge, who thoughtfully managed every step of the process.

I am also indebted to Sara Corbett, who read the adaptation with her customary care and sharp editorial mind, making many helpful suggestions.

This edition would not be possible without the entire

team at Delacorte Press/Random House Children's Books, especially publisher Beverly Horowitz. Thanks also to John Adamo, Dominique Cimina, Denise DeGennaro, Colleen Fellingham, Felicia Frazier, Rebecca Gudelis, Emily Harburg, Judith Haut, Erica Henegan, Noreen Herits, Tracy Heydweiller, Alison Kolani, Barbara Marcus, Stephanie Moss, Linda Palladino, Tamar Schwartz, Jinna Shin, Tim Terhune, and April Ward, as well as the marketing, publicity, sales, and foreign and subsidiary rights groups.

Finally, I would like to thank my family for the years of love, support, and learning they've provided me since this book was originally published. It's because of them that I will always feel young.

ABOUT THE AUTHOR

Barack Obama was the 44th president of the United States, elected in November 2008 and holding office for two terms. He is the author of the *New York Times* bestsellers *A Promised Land, Dreams from My Father,* and *The Audacity of Hope,* and is the recipient of the 2009 Nobel Peace Prize. He lives in Washington, D.C., with his wife, Michelle. They have two daughters, Malia and Sasha.